NOW IT'S YOUR TURN!

DANIEL AND ELISEA FRISHBERG

Edited by
SAL MONISTERE

ISBN:
978-1-68489-594-6

ISBN 978-168489594-6

DEDICATION

This Book is dedicated to Almighty God.

TABLE OF CONTENTS

Preface

One of the greatest honors of my life, was the opportunity to work closely for several years with the most accurate, insightful, and influential economist of the twentieth and twenty-first centuries.

Dr. Arthur Laffer almost singlehandedly brought the concepts of Supply Side Economics to the world of the 1970s and was a key factor in enabling Ronald Reagan to rescue American exceptionalism from the ten years of Presidential incompetence and mismanagement, that culminated in the Carter Administration.

I am just as proud today of his preface as I was when he wrote it ten years ago. I dedicate this edition of my most important work, to the great Dr. Arthur Laffer.

Daniel Frishberg

October 14, 2021

About the Author

Our country is extremely resilient and has withstood lots of hardship and deprivation and bounced back better than ever. In times like these the key is staying alive. Don't tell me about the return on my capital, I'm most interested in the return of my capital.

It is imperative to stay informed so that you can successfully navigate today's treacherous investment climate. And Daniel Frishberg can help you do just that. He has an uncanny ability to sense inflection points in the market, and in the pages that follow he lays out much of his view on what makes markets move. I've come to know Daniel and his wife Elisea very well over these past few years. So, before you jump in, let me tell you a little bit of what I know about Dan Frishberg.

I'll start by going all the way back to Daniel's routes in America. Dan's grand-fathers (maternal and paternal) came over from Russia at the beginning of the 20th century, generally to avoid the draft, which would have placed them both in the midst of the Czar's Army to fight the Russian Revolution. By the time Dan's maternal grandparents landed in America, there were restrictions already being placed on the immigrants who were coming to the United States and that, plus classes, left little time for a social life. The payoff was that he became one of the top students in the New York Community College system, and New York University found him and offered him a full and free scholarship to attend.

After college, Dan held jobs in advertising, homebuilding, and healthcare, but all the while he actively followed and participated in the markets. At the age of 40, Daniel met his future wife, Elisea, who challenged him to put his skills to full use and share them with others. She saw that he was bright, articulate, and energetic.

As for Elisea, she'd grown up in the Philippines and had not seen electricity until the age of 17. To say the least, they'd come from two different worlds. And so, this 25-year-old girl from the Philippines was the catalyst for the thought process that was then instilled in Dan Frishberg. He decided he'd begin sharing what he knew how to do with other people. At some point they were riding along in the car and Dan was complaining about something he'd just heard on the radio and how it didn't sound very smart to him. Elisea suggested he go on the radio himself and do a better job. His first reaction was, "I don't know anything about being on the radio ... but who knows? Maybe someday."

It wasn't long before Dan ended up back in the financial business. He went to work at Prudential Securities. Having learned the most interesting part of the money business on Wall Street, Dan was now learning what he felt was the most mundane part. But that little bit of conversation in the car that day about radio apparently sparked Dan somehow, because he ultimately ended up on the radio, doing a talk show (about money) in San Antonio. It was pretty much a first for the industry . . . there weren't a lot of financial shows on the air yet. Since then, the radio program has grown, as has the money management business Dan started on the side. This is where Dan began to see real opportunity.

First, to grow his radio concept into something the likes of which had not been seen before. People who knew nothing about Wall Street didn't realize that they were learning about it, all the while being entertained by the people presenting the information to them. Ask Dan Frishberg what he's doing these days and he'll answer without hesitation, "I'm having the time of my life."-

Dr.
Arthur Laffer

"Now, It's Your Turn!"

"Now, It's Your Turn"

It's our rallying cry. It's what we say to those who see our free market system as inherently unfair. They feel left out. Their parents or grandparents believed that America held great promise for them... all they had to do was contribute to the system and in return they would be justly and amply rewarded. But it's many of their descendants who find the system unfair.

Meanwhile, others of us are shocked and dismayed at those findings. We were taught in school and by our parents and grandparents that there's a direct connection between what we DO and what we GET.

We all share privileges earned by the heroes who fought and died to win and defend our way of life. We know we earn massive rewards by using our brains, courage and ingenuity to help people get what they want. But there's more to it than that... that's only the ante to get in the game.

This book is about how millionaires and billionaires get rich. How they use creative financing to multiply their money and make themselves rich. You're going to learn some new techniques here the likes of which you've never heard before. These less conventional techniques have always been reserved for the rich. Now, you're about to learn exactly what creative financing means, and how to apply it in your life.

Everyone should have an equal chance to be rich. And now, it's your turn.

Economics as we know it today is really all about the distinction between the rich and the poor. And most of the world sees them as two competing groups. In fact, many think of this distinction as two different species – there are rich people, and then there are poor people, and those who see things this way think you were born as one or the other. They don't realize that you can change from one to the other.

They believe this competition suggests that if one of them gets something, the other has to lose something. Of course, they're wrong. They're missing out on the chance to change their family's lives forever. And that's why I'm writing this book… so that you can move from a world where you're stuck, into a world where you can create the life you want.

They also see the world as a competition for scarce resources. In other words, if I have these resources, you can't get them because there's a limited supply. It's the basis for a lot of the political problems we have. It's not just in the U.S.: think of the issues they have in Russia, China and other places where communism is prevalent. They see competition for scarce resources. There's not enough of 'em, and when you get them, I don't. They don't see an ability to create more resources, or that wealth is a reward for creating more resources.

Back in the 19th century, everyone in the world believed in the Malthusian theory. It said that we were approaching the limit to the number of people the Earth could support, that there wasn't going to be enough food, there wouldn't be enough resources. That defined the limit or extent of the world's population. This justified why people should compete for resources, and why countries should go to war, and why individuals should try to keep others down in order to get more for themselves. It was their belief in scarcity.

As you know, the world's population has increased dramatically since then. The solution we discovered was innovation and creativity. We found new technologies and new ways to create food and new ways to create resources. And now everyone knows there's an infinite supply of resources; we're not even close to maxing out.

These new inventions and new technologies come from a special ability that human beings have that no other animal has. True, we've inherited most of our characteristics from animals, from mammals like the apes, and yet we have what nobody else has. We can see and act on things that we know deep in our own minds, even if they're not visible. We make conclusions and create new inventions; we think of ways to do things that were never done before. We create new tools that never existed. It's our ability to know there are solutions even when we can't see them.

As recently as twenty years ago, there was a theory that was advanced by a guy who became very famous, whose name was Matt Simmons. I used to have him on my radio program often, and he was the most successful and well-paid analyst in the oil business. He believed that we were hitting Peak Oil about fifteen or twenty years back. Peak Oil referred to the idea that we were exploiting all the resources on the planet, that there was a finite amount, and that we'd be limited. It was kind of the Malthusian theory about resources. The solution called for a new invention, a new idea.

That invention we now know of is called fracking. They figured out that there was a lot of oil trapped in the stone beneath the surface of the earth, down in the porous rock. And they figured out that if they'd drill down and pour water into it, the pressure of the water would crack the rock open. This freed enormous amounts of oil and gas that nobody ever dreamed were there. Today we know that we're only just beginning to scratch the surface of these resources.

Again, the solution was figuring out something that nobody had ever thought of before. Something they couldn't really see, yet they knew it was there. The solution was pointed out by my old friend and mentor, Art Laffer. By the way, he was the guy who kind of invented Reaganomics and a cure for the destructive society that we had in the 1970's - runaway inflation and not enough of anything for everybody. Reagan became president when just a couple of years earlier, nobody ever dreamed Ronald Reagan could be the president.

But the destruction that happened from this belief of scarcity in the Carter administration resulted in Ronald Reagan's election victory. Arthur Laffer understood this and told me very early that the answer to all these problems that human beings have can be solved with technology.

It's been the impetus for our species to explore the rest of the universe. The solution to our problems - running out of space, time, or anything else – is that we're at the very rudimentary beginning of that exploration. But it's become pretty clear that we're never going to run out of space, and we're never going to run out of resources.

In this book, we're going to talk about how you can develop the ability that you were born with, the ability to make a difference in your life. Yes, you do have it, but you have to be able to put it to work.

Here's a perfect example; a couple of years ago, I visited Las Vegas - this is after the onslaught of COVID. Everybody stopped traveling, tourism was down. Then I went back shortly thereafter, and it was beginning to get crowded again. I looked around and I saw that one of the most underestimated places there was the MGM Grand. (A little later in this book, I'm going to tell you a story about how that company came to be).

As I say, the crowds were coming back but they had only recovered to about half of what they were before COVID. But I saw that MGM was creating all kinds of different entertainment hotels, different levels of quality, different levels of luxury, and some novelty ideas. Everywhere you looked in the fanciest locations was another MGM hotel.

They were cool places, and they were becoming crowded with happy people having a ball. I started to do some research. I found that they too, were about halfway back to the revenues that they were used to earning, because Las Vegas in general was only about halfway back to the money they earned pre-COVID.

I looked at MGM's plans for expansion and marketing, and I noticed they were taking a big position in the gambling business. They already had a deal to provide the electronic gambling for Buffalo Wild Wings. As various states in the U.S began to legalize sports gambling, MGM was making deals with restaurants and bars to be the software provider for gambling. This is MGM, OK?

Now, there's another very stylish company focused on Millennials that's called Draft Kings, but they have no history of returning profits to anybody. To me, it's like betting on numbers with the Sopranos or something. But MGM is in this gambling niche in addition to building out these fabulous, fun properties. They have properties in Macau, which is like the Las Vegas of China (but bigger), as well as in Singapore. By the way, these countries had also been seeing reduced tourism and reduced travel.

But I saw that MGM was very well placed, setting themselves up to do all this electronic gambling, and they had all these fabulous hotels, and they were poised to recover. Meanwhile, their stock was way down - I talked about this a lot on radio and television. Of course, there were all kinds of obstacles and bad news about COVID. And along comes a new variant. And there are some people who can't get the vaccines, and nothing is working. There was all kinds of bad news that was delaying the recovery from COVID.

I figured that owning stock in MGM was an absolute path to wealth. And I used some techniques to get a very high leverage position to own a lot of MGM with just a little bit of money - techniques that you're going to learn about in this book.

I told a lot of people about it, and the stock just sort of fluctuated for a year. Back when I bought it (June of 2020), it was about $16 a share. And then it went up. It hadn't even been announced that there was a COVID vaccine yet, but I was sure that we were going to get past that... I was making all kinds of bets on what was going to happen as the world recovered. I knew that the answer to this was going to be technology. And I knew that we were going to get past it, we were going to figure it out, figure out how to beat COVID.

So back in June of 2020, MGM stock was at $16, I was saying that it was certain that we were going to get past COVID, and the stock ended up going to about twenty- five dollars. I suspected before anybody knew there was a cure, that we were finding ways to treat COVID.

There were different advances going on. A lot of people had confidence that humans were going to figure out the solution to this influenza just like we figured out everything else. The stock was up to $25. And then it crashed. Because of COVID, the summer ended with a loss of confidence. The recovery was irregular, and like Las Vegas traffic, the tourist and gambling business backed up. The people that were watching the earnings of this company had seen it grow from $16 to $25 - and now it was falling back. Tourism was down and the stock was down. It looked like a big loser and lots of people gave up.

I'm writing this about a year and a half later, and the stock today, in the autumn of 2021, is at forty-five! Forty-five dollars! And you'll come to understand that this happens all the time and how to take advantage of it using the leverage that you're going to learn about in this book. They're new techniques that you have maybe never tried before, but the rich have been using them for ten or fifteen years now.

In a little over a year and a half, investors who had purchased the acquisition rights to buy stock in MGM (for just a couple of bucks each) made twenty times their investment. Unfortunately, and this is the real lesson here, most of the people that heard about this never got there because they couldn't see past that day's news report. When they heard tourism was down, they sold the stock, and there were more sellers than buyers. And MGM stock went down. And they got disappointed. And they gave up. And they sold out. And I can't tell you how many people told me that MGM was the biggest losing idea they had ever heard from me.

Friends, these are people that have been listening to me on the radio for twenty-five years. People I helped to make a fortune. And they said this is the biggest loser they ever got from me and they gave up. And here, a year and a half later, MGM stock is at forty-five, they're building hotels everywhere, and making huge profits on gaming and gambling.

Their Macau properties are doing great. Their Singapore properties are doing great. The people who didn't give up, those who used the techniques you're going to learn about in this book, they made as much as twenty times their money in a year and a half. $10,000 turned into $200,000 in a year and a half. This is how people get rich. Those people that said it was just a big loser gave up because of what they could only see. They just couldn't see past the news of the day.

Animals see what is. But the most developed human beings see what can be. You have to use the faculty of acting on what you know, not on what you see. Now to help you understand this, I want to examine consciousness. I first learned about this at NYU, and it changed my life and it made me millions. And that's what this book is going to do for you if you allow it to. What I've studied about the advent of consciousness inspired me to use my highest level of consciousness whenever I thought about it – it didn't come naturally, I have to force myself to do it.

The Evolution of Man

In the early days of our planet there were life's simplest forms, one-celled organisms and amoebas, and all of the other primitive plants and one-celled animals. But let's jump ahead to the jellyfish, nothing more than a community of cells. The jellyfish had the ability to sense when you touch it, the jellyfish could see light and hear sound. But it couldn't put these things together; there was nothing to organize all these stimuli. No plan, no understanding, no consciousness.

Moving forward, millions of years of evolution pass. These beings begin to advance and here come the reptiles. Now you have an alligator, and that alligator can see. It's got eyes just like the jelly fish and it sees, and it hears, and it feels. But it also has this rudimentary way of integrating sight and sound and feeling, and from that it can plan. Just imagine that alligator saying to himself, 'I'm going to move to another part of the pond where there are fewer alligators, and I can get more food". It can actually make that plan. It can see a critter on the bank and say, "I think I could catch that critter and have it for dinner". Now that's far and above what the jellyfish could do, so the alligator was a more resourceful and successful being.

Let's jump ahead in time again. We're at roughly sixty-five million years ago, when the big reptiles (the dinosaurs) ruled our planet. They were huge and strong. But they were cold blooded, just like any reptile. And suddenly, the weather changed. It was the beginning of the Ice Age. The dinosaurs had the ability to decide how to get food, but only at a very rudimentary level; they didn't have an advanced brain. They could only organize what they could see and feel... but they couldn't figure out what to do. And once the weather got cold, well... we all know what became of the dinosaurs, right?

Time marches on. It's now the age of the mammals, previously banished and hiding behind the trees (from the dinosaurs). They developed an ability to think things through. They continued to adapt. They began to hide in caves. And the most important thing they learned was to move to another area when the need arose. They moved to warmer places. They learned to climb trees to keep safe (just in case those pesky dinosaurs should come back), and they became the most successful animals that had ever existed on the planet – they ruled the planet.

Mammals still rule the world. They see, they smell, they hear, and they react. They eat as necessary, or they run away when they see danger. A great example is the squirrel. They plan for the winter - they save up nuts for the winter. Human beings, though, evolved into something that nobody had ever seen before. We developed an ability to imagine something that wasn't there, and even used that ability to imagine new methods of getting food.

As a matter of fact, about 10,000 years ago, somebody recognized the idea that the food they were eating was replenishing itself and growing. They figured out how to cultivate, how to get the seeds from the crop and replant them to make more crops. They saw that killing the bad surrounding plants would allow the good crops to grow even bigger and better... and produce more seeds. It was the dawn of agriculture, something that nobody had ever seen before.

Humans can invent things. Monkeys have the same eyes and ears as we do, and even a brain - but they still live the same way their ancestors did 30,000 years ago. Humans invent. We see things in our minds that aren't yet there, we're able to put ideas together, realize things that we can't see. And this advance led us to do things that no other animal has ever done before.

So here we are, back in the present. People around us are hearing all kinds of horrible news... everything is going wrong. The news media has replaced the word of mouth that once existed in small villages. Those media naturally want a bigger audience, and they've learned that the audience responds to horrible news about things like COVID. They broadcast more and more bad news, more and more danger. Yet opportunities continue to present themselves. Now if we use our ability to think about things we know, that we can't yet see, then we can create and take advantage of opportunities that are developing.

You know, four billion people in this world don't have electricity. Half the people in the world have never seen ice cream! What I know is that over the next ten or twenty years, the whole world is going to benefit from artificial intelligence, they're going to advance, using things that we've invented here in the United States - they're already seeing things that they've never seen before.

They're watching television, they're watching us on their cell phones, they're watching Netflix, and they're seeing us living a life that's so much easier and more convenient, and more luxurious, and more comfortable, and more plentiful than the world they live in. But you know, they're also using that inherent human faculty - they're inventive people who can see things, who are able to think of things they can't yet see, and they're imagining how the people in their country can get what we already have.

This is already happening. These people are going to learn to live like we do. But as they buy the inventions and methods that were invented by us, we're going to profit from them. Maybe you see the people who act on what they see, rising inflation, shortages of manufacturing, shortages of computer chips, new Delta variants, and all kinds of stuff. But I see a world where four or five billion people need and want things that we've invented. And I'm going to make a fortune owning the companies that bring that new world to them. And you can do the same.

Eventually, if you decide to use your mammal faculties, acting on what you see, hear and feel, you're going to end up like the other mammals, like squirrels. You'll spend your life hiding from danger and storing a little bit at a time. And maybe because you do it a little more efficiently than a squirrel, and you create a little bit more surplus, you'll have a little bit of leisure time when you're eighty. Working and saving and working and saving. But then what? Here you are near the end of your life; you're still poor and your family is still poor, and you still live in a mediocre neighborhood and your kids see other people's kids going to great schools and living in great neighborhoods.

This is basically the savings plan that you learned from your financial planner. Accumulate through savings a little bit of your meager paycheck, a paycheck you get from somebody else who has wealth, power, leisure, and freedom and who is exploiting you. This is why you should resent him, rather than buying in and emulating him. Here's how you become that guy that you work for. It's the story about consciousness. Let's talk about how we've been able to apply that higher level of consciousness.

THE STORY OF BIG RED

The Story of Big Red

You know, there's a guy I really have to admire. I met him when I lived in San Antonio, Texas. His name is Red McCombs, and he's really a very smart guy who sells cars. He's also been an owner in the NBA, the NFL, and a lot of other very lucrative ventures. But he actually became one of the richest people in the world by selling cars. He's helped select a car, then get the money to finance the car, if it breaks, he helps get it repaired, he does all of it. That's his business, he's very good at it, and he's gotten rich.

But cycles run everywhere. Some people postponed buying a car today because maybe they didn't feel well, or they were afraid to get COVID. Or maybe it looked like rain, or whatever. But Red knows it will cycle back up and he'll be fine. And do you know why nobody buys stock in Red McCombs' car company? It's because he doesn't need your money, so he doesn't let you buy in. You can buy a car from him, or you can be part of the cycle that postpones buying it for now, but Red knows that eventually you're going to need a car. He's a great car salesman, no doubt.

I bring up Red McCombs name and I'll use him in the following example, but I'm pretty sure the same thinking was at play when Tom Benson got rich, another car dealer from Texas. He ended up owning the New Orleans Saints, the basketball team, racehorses, and a good-sized part of Louisiana. It probably applies to the big car dealer in your area too. But I think it's important for you know how Red got rich in the first place.

Think about this. He had some money, and he wanted to sell cars, right? But he only had a certain amount of money, not enough to buy the necessary inventory. So he went to Ford and said "Look, I'm going to open this dealership here. I'm very good at selling. I'm spending my own money on the land, but I want you to advance me the cars. And I want you to give me the right to pay you when I sell them, at a price we agree on today... and it can even be a little more than if I had to pay on delivery, OK?"

Well, that allowed him to immediately have hundreds of cars on his lot when he really didn't have the money to buy hundreds of cars. Because he'd pay extra for the acquisition rights to those cars, they advanced him enough cars to fill up that lot. And he advertised and built a big business. And he became a multi-millionaire, which he never could have done if he just used the money that he had. But by buying the acquisition rights to those cars he was able to defer his payment to Ford until somebody came in and bought the car. All he did was figure out how to make a deal with Ford. He got to do it on a much bigger scale than he could have had he not done that deal. Because he's smart.

Now, do you have someone who'll advance you a deal like that so you can make a lot of money? I'll remind you that if you're an idiot, you'll get transfixed on guessing how many people are going to buy cars this month; you'll focus on whether it rains or not, or if people are getting the vaccine, or whatever. And if you'd been able to actually get shares in Red's company and you're really not thinking, you'd sell off those shares because you're worried it might rain a lot this month, or something similar that might keep people from going out to buy a car right now. You're focused on the cycle, not the way the company has been structured.

So much of our way of life is structured. These rich car dealers keep showing cars and keep getting richer, because they know that people have a structural need to buy cars. The cycle – whether they buy this month or next month –

doesn't matter. He knows how many people there are and he knows there's this structural need to have a car to get to work. He knows that as the car wears out, they're gonna have to be repaired or replaced. And he's not going to use cash now, because he's already set up this sweet deal with Ford.

So next he decides he wants to own a Hyundai dealership or maybe some other kind of dealership - he wants all of them. So he goes to each of those car companies and asks for the acquisition rights to a bunch of cars. And those manufacturers agree to the same deal he has with Ford. And he just keeps doing it because he's figured it out. He bought options with Ford, with Hyundai, and a lot more. And he keeps getting richer. I guess it's too bad you and I can't own a piece of his dealerships, but as I said, he really doesn't need our money.

But you know what? We can own shares in the steel company that mines the iron, turns it into sheets of steel and sells them to the car companies. And we can make great money because that steel is also going to go into making rebar to build roads and bridges, and to build high rises in Africa and India. We can't own stock in Red McCombs car dealership... but we can own the companies that make the cars or the parts for the cars... we can own that. And every time one of those car dealers sells a car, they'll need more steel. How about that?

Of course you know that as the world recovers from COVID, more people are going to buy cars, and more people are going to be on the road. And we're going to fix the roads, so we'll need steel for that as well as for those car parts. Do you want to think rich, or you want to think poor? Some people are focused on the news, the cyclical ups and downs, the shiny objects, and they seldom get anywhere except by luck.

Yes, I'll admit it… some people get lucky playing slot machines. Some people get lucky guessing the cycles. Me? I'm optimizing, I'm not guessing the cycle. I'm learning to use acquisition rights to make myself rich, because I'm going to own the steel company that mines the iron and turns it into steel for the car company. And you know what? I'm not just buying the stock of the steel company. I'm buying acquisition rights to the steel company just as the car dealer did with Ford. It's exactly the same concept.

I'm Going to Make Sure You Get Your Turn

I can tell you that a couple of years ago, I wasn't that worried about whether you could 'think rich and be rich'. I was living on the beach in Florida, with gorgeous weather and gorgeous sunsets, and to me, that was really living. And we were just investing our own money exactly the way we're talking about here. But we weren't even thinking about how 'the ninety-five percent' were investing - I was focused on rich people, because I was a money manager. And if you didn't have a lot of money, you couldn't really pay me enough to manage your money. I mean, I was only getting one or two percent a year for providing that management, so I couldn't really afford to do it for everyone.

At that time, I wasn't even thinking about you so much. But we were watching the news a couple of years ago and watching the world in a downward spiral… people talking about how things are not fair. They go to college and nobody's teaching them how to make money there. And they think it's suddenly all not fair.

That's when my wife, Elisea said that we should try to do something about this. We can stop this erosion of the country and help these people who are going out and angrily protesting because they're not being included. We can help them get included. We can devote our lives to teaching people how to do this. And that's what we're doing. I've happily changed my focus to care whether you get rich or not. So I'd like to help you. Look, a lot of other people have used the same trick that Red McCombs used buying acquisition rights to make his money go much further.

I had an inkling of this idea years ago, and here's how the idea came about. It's similar to the story of Red McCombs. Here's a guy named Kirk Kerkorian. He's in Las Vegas, just out of the Air Force at the end of World War Two. Now even though he'd quit school in the eighth grade, he was smart. He bought a bunch of surplus Air Force bombers and was using them to transport cargo. And he was starting to make a little bit of money.

Very nearby, was the real Las Vegas – the Strip and all the nice casinos and all the traffic. And he got this idea. There was this beautiful parcel of land out by McCarran airport, and there were a couple of things starting to be built there. But there was plenty of room for growth, so he went to the people who owned about eighty acres of land right along the Las Vegas Strip. This is just after WWII... there was very little.

He made a deal, just as Red McCombs had. He bought the acquisition rights to the land. He said to them, I want the right to buy this acreage from you for a million dollars, but I'm not going to buy it right now. I'm going to give you $200,000 now and I want you to give me the exclusive right to buy it from you later for a million dollars.

So with that deal in hand, he forms a company. He personally buys acquisition rights to thirty percent of that company, which ultimately became MGM, right? Then, because he's got the acquisition rights, he uses it to raise money to build hotels on that land... in fact he raises thirty million dollars. Now he's got the acquisition right to own thirty percent of the company, so he's already worth nine million... and he hadn't even built anything yet!

Kerkorian did all this just because he was smart. He used his brain and took options on that land, and now he's worth $9 million dollars, and he raises enough money to build the International Hotel there on the strip. And then he builds the MGM Grand and is then worth tons and tons of money. Wait… there's more. Allow me if you will, to take you a little farther down the path of success with this guy. He had another idea.

He loved movies, and he wanted to be in the movie business, right? So he goes to Hollywood, and he finds this guy who's written a script for a hit movie, and gives the guy a few thousand dollars for the exclusive right to buy that script. With that deal in hand, he cuts a deal with Clark Gable and some other celebrities to be in his movie.

Then he runs out and raises enough money to make that movie! He's got a great script, he's got Clark Gable, and he's finishing construction on his new MGM Studios. And he makes the movie and makes yet another ton of money. And when he died, he died worth sixteen billion dollars. All by doing deals like that, using his brain to do exactly what our friend Red McCombs did. Pretty amazing, yes?

Options Work That Way, Too

These rich guys did it, which stimulated me to do the same exact thing. Let me tell you how options work exactly the same way as buying acquisition rights. So here's Freeport McMoRan, a big copper mining company. And the stock is at $37 per share. Let's say I've got 20 grand - that's not really enough money to make me rich. That would buy me 540 shares. But I'd own $20,000 worth of a company that's going to help people all over India get electricity and change people's lives, etc.

But, but, but… I could buy the acquisition rights to buy those shares at forty two dollars each for $2.20 per share. Now that doesn't let me own the share. It gives me the acquisition rights to those shares. I know the shares are going to be worth more later, and with my twenty thousand dollars I can buy the acquisition rights to 9090 shares of Freeport McMoran stock right now. I'll have the exclusive right to buy those particular shares for $42. Granted, the stock is only at thirty-seven dollars, but I know that stock's going to be worth more money.

Now somebody's asking uh, why would I buy the right to get it at forty-two when I could buy it for thirty-seven right now? The answer is, I'm buying a bunch of them for $2.20 each. I'm buying 9090 shares of Freeport McMoran, not 540 shares. That means a little guy with twenty grand could own $336,363 (9090x37) worth of a company that's changing people's lives by selling copper and allowing them to wire houses in India. Optimizing means more power from your money to make a difference. Instead of $20,000 worth of a company, making a little bit of money, I have $336,000 worth of that company, and I'm changing more people's lives and making a bigger difference. That's how it works.

Remember That 'Red' Guy?

I didn't make this up - Red McCombs and Kirk Kerkorian figured it out. And since we're on a roll here with stories of the rich and famous, I want to tell you one more, about how the Hunt brothers got so rich. They're some of the richest people in the world, and they did it essentially the same way.

They heard about this guy named Slaughter who back in the 1870's saw bubbles coming up in the San Jacinto River up near the Houston airport, up near Humble. He figured there might be oil there. Now he was running around, hot on the idea of his discovery, but he couldn't get anybody to pay any attention to him. And he was afraid to show people with money where the oil was, because then what would they need him for, right?

Jump ahead thirty years to the turn of the century, around 1900, when they found oil in a salt dome in Beaumont, Texas, just a couple of hours to the east. They found big gushers of oil. Suddenly people started to realize - hey, we have salt domes like this in Houston. And just as suddenly, the land that was $16 an acre is selling for $250,000 an acre and nobody can afford to buy it. Ah, but this very smart guy in Austin figures he could do that same trick by buying rights. So he goes to Humble, Texas and says to the people who owned the land, "Look, I can't buy your land - you can maintain ownership. But I'll give you a third of my drilling company in exchange for the exclusive right to drill for oil on your land".

Now that he's got the exclusive right to drill on the land, he's putting the resources together. He's got the right to drill. The people that own the land are happy that they're gonna get royalties forever, right? But he has a company and now he's running around to raise the money to do the drilling. It's money from a few very smart people. And they find exactly the same gushers there in those salt domes, just as they did in Beaumont.

Now, the grandfather of H.L. Hunt didn't really have any money. He's over in Fort Worth when he hears about this. He takes some money that he won playing poker, and he runs around all over East Texas, from Houston all the way to Louisiana. And he buys… guess what? Exclusive acquisition rights. He gives people a share of the company for the exclusive right to drill on their land. He locks up all that land in East Texas and became one of the richest people in the world. And we can turn profits too. Last year Freeport McMoran turned $10,000 into $300,000. All by using the exact same trick that those guys use. I hope you're taking notes.

Roku and Peanut Butter

When my son was in college, he was a baseball player, and was otherwise very involved in sports. When he came home on a break or on weekends, he wanted to watch football games on TV. Well at the time, I had Direct TV and I could watch almost anything, but it was expensive, as I recall a few hundred dollars a month. And it was my son who told me about some new gadget called Roku. They had a little device that you could buy at Best Buy for twenty-nine dollars. You plug it into the back of your TV, and it becomes a streaming receiver - and I could get virtually any game we wanted to see. And except for those twenty-nine dollars, it cost nothing!

So, I bought that to indulge my son, although I was pretty sure I was going to keep my Direct TV. But once we got that Roku, I could watch anything I wanted, so I realized I had no need to hang onto the Direct TV. And within a week I had gotten rid of it. And I knew that this was going to spread around the world. Receiving television digitally - this is a real digital transformation!

And what I didn't realize about Roku is it was all aimed at the advertisers. They could advertise on these programs that were being broadcast over Roku, which is virtually everything. They also tell how many people were seeing their ads. And they could program it in such a way that if I had been searching online for a new car, they could actually program their advertising to reach people like me, or other people who had searched for the things they wanted. Roku is a fabulous new thing.

In fact, you don't even need to spend the twenty-nine dollars anymore because television manufacturers all over the world are incorporating Roku software right into the box. And you probably have a digital television or 'Smart TV' that includes the Roku operating system... the same system that I plugged into the back of my TV, but the twenty-nine dollars is already built into the cost of your

TV. I knew right there and then that Roku was going to spread everywhere, that it was just a better digital way of doing things.

Speaking of my son, because he was a baseball player, he was a quite a health nut. He was eating a lot of peanut butter, and he realized that he couldn't get to all the peanut butter because he couldn't get to the bottom of the jar. So as a part of an assignment in his business class, he came up with this idea for a peanut butter jar that had a screw-on top on the top… and a screw-on bottom on the bottom. I know. Simple, right?

Well, he thought it was a clever idea and so he had a prototype made on a 3-D printer to make an actual jar that did what he wanted. He was at Loyola University in New Orleans, and he presented the idea to a local TV station that carried 'Shark Tank'. There was a competition on locally and he won! In fact, he won $1,000. So he calls me and says, "Dad, I'm trying to make a little spending money by driving for Uber. But I just picked up $1000, and I'd like to do some day trading… will you teach me how?"

I told him that day trading is not for smart people, and that it doesn't really work that well. Day traders are looking for an easy way to do things and most of them don't really get anywhere with it. They make money, but they also lose money, because people don't operate in patterns. I told him I'd teach him a way to really make real money. And what I taught him is essentially what I'm talking to you about here in this book.

We bought an option on Roku stock, a long term, multi-year option. By the way, that's very much like what Roku gives to its employees. In order to save money on the employees, they allow them to sign on to a stock accumulation plan. They got that idea from Microsoft and other digital companies. So the employees at Roku can sign on to this stock accumulation plan and they get stock options. And what happens is, as the stock is worth more and more money, the employees get rich (like the employees at Microsoft), and everybody knows that if you work at Microsoft for ten or twenty years, you retire as a multimillionaire. That can easily happen when a part of your pay comes in stock options, and the stock is continually worth more money. Those options allow you to own large amounts of the company, because you have the right to buy the company.

So I showed my son Larry how to do that by buying options on Roku. And that was the very beginning. He started to make money, and he came back and said, "You know I have some friends that are trying to day trade and they're not getting anywhere. They make money, and then they lose it back. Can you teach them how to do this?" So I did. And after a while, a couple of his friends called me and said, you know, you can make money teaching this, people would be willing to pay for this. And I said, Okay, bring me some students and I'll teach them my 5-step class, and I'll give you a commission. (I had been on a cruise and learned about affiliate fees). Anyway, there's a little personal back history about my son and me.

(The 5-Step Class)

By the way, I still teach that class today, and it teaches five steps, which I'll detail for you a little later. But for now, here are the steps: You learn to identify the right companies, to evaluate them, to acquire the company in the best way, then to monitor it, and the big number five, to take profits off the table.

WHY ISN'T EVERYONE USING THE "OPTIONS METHOD"?

Why isn't Everyone Using "The Options Method"?

I want to talk for a minute about why this powerful tool - acquisition rights to a valuable appreciating asset - isn't being used ubiquitously. Why isn't this tool taught in basic finance classes or by fathers to their promising teenage children?

It's because this valuable technique uses options, which are available on credible regulated exchanges. But the word 'options' scares most of the people who would benefit from learning about them. In trying to be conservative, they succeed in missing an opportunity for unlimited gains, with sharply limited losses – clearly a risk reduction technique.

The acquisition rights that are so useful to me - and to you with some minimal training - employ multi-year options, which lock in very inexpensive contractual rights to acquire appreciating assets, at fixed prices, years in the future. They enable us to hold onto these assets for years without tying up much of our scarce capital.

These options, though, are also available with expiration dates of a month or two, and even a week or two. They are used by risk prone gamblers to make bets on how much a stock or other asset may go up or down in the next couple of weeks, or in a month or two.

Of course, anybody with a lick of common sense knows that these gamblers really have no way to know what the price of a certain asset will do over the next few weeks or months. Markets and stock prices fluctuate erratically over any short period of time.

On the other hand, we know that if a company sells more and profits rise, the company is more valuable to its owners, and its stock price will reflect that increased value. Over time, this happens - 100% of the time!

In other words, a company whose sales and profits are rising will always eventually see long-term appreciation, even though none of us have any idea what will happen to the stock price over the next week, month, or even year. Young people, who are notorious for copying each other and following trends, use these short-term options as gambling devices to try to guess what the stock price will be on assets they know very little about.

From our point of view, there is nothing wrong with gambling at the casino or at the racetrack. I acknowledge that some people find this fun, but clearly, blackjack and horse races are not investments for the players, but only for the owners of the casino or the track.

These kids generally end up losing their money, eventually, as do most gamblers. Accordingly, the options they use are known to be highly risky. On the other hand, contracting for the right to acquire an appreciating asset, years in the future is a highly reliable way to make a lot of money, even though the tool they use has the same name.

A simple analogy can clarify this distinction.
The automobile was a fabulous invention that made our lives much better immediately. It made it possible for us to get to work economically and safely and made travel easy and affordable. As cars became easier to drive and more powerful, teenagers started to use them to express their machismo and virility

by sneaking off to deserted roads and drag racing. Of course, this gave rise to unnecessary accidents and even deaths.

It would be a foolish mistake to conclude that the automobile is a dangerous invention and should be avoided. Cars are a wonderfully useful tool when used intelligently, but because they are powerful, abusing them can give rise to undesirable outcomes.

In the same way, using multi-year options as an inexpensive way to contract for the right to acquire an appreciating asset is a very powerful technique that can change your financial life forever. Using short term options as a gambling device to bet on the price of assets you know little or nothing about is… well, forgive my candor, but it's just plain stupid. It isn't the tool that is dangerous, it is the foolish abuser.

MasterCard (Please Insert Your Card Now)

The economy runs into all kinds of temporary obstacles – it speeds up, it slows down, and people buy or sell their stocks according to the news of the day, or the mood of the moment. In reality, it doesn't matter what happens this day, week or month. In fact, it makes no difference if the world takes another year or two to get over these worries. Mastercard is going to be integral to growth and rebuilding around the world. The company will be worth much more money in the future than it is worth right now. I can't see this, but I know it. Herein lies the opportunity. The stock is going down, while the prospects for Mastercard profits are fabulous and soaring.

MasterCard is a company that doesn't lend money to anybody. But they do have a brilliant system that lets people worldwide plug in and conduct business with each other, as though they were living together in a little tiny village, and it uses technology that was developed right here in America.

This "American" way of conducting commerce will spread everywhere over the next ten years, and as it does, Mastercard's revenues, profits and value are almost certain to rise accordingly. The company value increases. It's a sure thing to happen, so what kind of a fool would be willing to sell the stock at this point?

The answer is, 99% of investors are willing to sell the stock, because they see everyone else selling it, and they really don't understand the company or why it's valuable. They bought it because the herd was buying it. Then, they sold it because the herd was selling it. How wonderful to be playing against them.

I didn't invent MasterCard, but I knew it was a winner. And I knew it was growing around the world. And I knew the more money it made, the more valuable ownership shares were. And you knew this too. I also knew that our highly developed economic system would allow me to buy rights to own MasterCard instead of buying the stock itself. First, I learned that I could be an owner of MasterCard, and then, just as you're learning here, I learned that I could own a bigger piece of it - all simply by using my brain to get a better deal.

The irony is, you knew all the same things, you knew them three years ago, and you still know them now.

Let's go back to February 2017. Now, you'll have to imagine a chart that shows all of this, but MasterCard stock was at $108. If I had $1,000, I could have bought nine shares of stock. But if I used the same technique I'd showed to my son about Roku, I could buy an option - I could buy the rights to acquire that stock later at an agreed-upon price. So for $1.52 per share option, I buy the right to acquire that stock later for $130. And you're asking me why on earth would I want that stock later for $130, when I could easily buy it now for $108?

Well, remember, I'm only paying $1.52 per share for the option. So I could buy more than 60 times as much of it.

Stay with me. I'd own a very big piece of that company. By paying only $1.52 a share, I could have the right to buy a whole lot more of that stock for a much bigger piece of the pie. And if you're asking me how on Earth I could buy it for just $1.52, it's because very, very few people were thinking about buying that stock later for $130. There was no real demand for that, and few people understood the technique.

So back to my chart, it's now about a year later. In January 2018 that stock had gone up from $108 to $166. But remember, I had my option to buy it for $130. I could exercise my option to buy it for $130 and sell it for $166. So that option was worth $36 - in real money. Let that sink in… in just one year, I turned $1.52 into $36! Think about that!

I really liked the idea of using a little leverage, and I wanted to own more and more of MasterCard. I bought another option that allowed me the right to buy that stock at $210. And again, you ask, why do you want an option to buy it at $210 when you can get it now for $166? And again, it's because I know that MasterCard is going to be worth a lot more, and yes, I want an even bigger share of that company.

So I take my profits and I buy the option to acquire it for $210 at some future date. (By the way, this option is now going to cost me about $3). That stock had gone from $166 to $202. I took my money and I bought the option to buy it later for $260. Guess what happened in January of 2020. MasterCard stock was at $323!!

As you know, MasterCard's prospects are only improving, while the world of mammals has not caught on yet and is presently selling the stock. The bargain continues to be available. We will get to do the same gambit again, maybe multiple times.

You are now joining the people who use their higher brain function, and can act on what they know, instead of what they see and hear – and we are inheriting the world.

There's a Billionaire Inside You...

The introduction to my radio show says there's a billionaire locked inside you, and that the key to freedom is information. Let me explain how that billionaire got there, and how he/she is going to change your life - if you let him or her. There's a lot to discuss here, because the world is in an uproar, and frankly, it doesn't make any sense. In fact, it's providing us with an unbelievably good and very lucrative opportunity. That's because there's so much crazy stuff going on in the world, driving down the stock prices of companies that are going to make a fortune with rising sales and rising profits - at least a decade of growing profits ahead of them. And yet, their stock prices are falling. They're being sold as I'm writing this today.

COVID is putting a stop to everything. Right now (in the fall of 2021) we have supply chain backups, the economy is weakening – and prices for goods and services are going up.

People are worried - they feel a lot of inflation; they feel that the value of their money and their savings is in decline. That's happening because they feel like they're surrounded by incompetence. They watched the president and his administration get intimidated by a little country like Afghanistan. They've seen so much mismanagement, so much foolish stuff and so much of a misunderstanding of economics that they can't help being worried.

But as I'm writing this, the whole COVID thing is getting better. Fewer and fewer people are getting it. About 75 or 80% of Americans have been vaccinated for COVID and a lot of them have been vaccinated twice. And now we're developing a booster so that there's really no cause for future worry about it. Now the media announce the fact that you may have to get a booster for COVID every year. Oh my God, what a horrible negative. You know, I get a booster every year for pneumonia and the flu from the VA, and I never thought of that as 'negative'. In fact, I think it's great.

You see, these viruses have always been able to evolve faster than our drug companies could come up with vaccines. They develop a vaccine, and after a while the vaccine doesn't work anymore. The viruses evolve faster than we've been able to come up with new medicines. But now, our drug companies use artificial intelligence to do their research. And they're fast; Artificial Intelligence is so fast, it does calculations in tiny fractions of a second. And for the first time in history, we're coming up with cures faster than these viruses can evolve.

What's the big negative deal about having viruses around anyway? Viruses are tiny little micro-organisms. There are viruses, there are bacteria, there are all kinds of things out there. Heck, there are lions and tigers, but the bottom line is, we can handle any and all of it. And here in America, we really don't have a big problem with the flu or pneumonia. Those things infect a lot of people, and they could be lethal. But we have vaccines, so why all the negativities? I don't know. But I know that what's happening is the mere fear of COVID is causing a lot of things to come to a stop.

For now, a lot of people don't want to go to work, because they're getting all kinds of free money. But in addition, they watch and listen to all the news and they're afraid that if they go to work, they're going to be exposed to COVID. And they're going to get it! And many are afraid to take the vaccine because there are side effects. It's all created quite an illusion of a dangerous situation.

The biggest reason is because the media is our main method of transferring information from one human being to another in our society. We used to live in little towns or villages… now we're one gigantic village with 350 million people, communicating with others we can't even see. We share the same worldview and the same information because the transmission mechanism is the media - radio, television, and the internet. If the media all say things often enough, and enough people repeat it, then everyone begins to believe it. For all intents and purposes, it becomes reality for all of us.

The fact is the media don't really try to transmit the truth. I can tell you this from having worked in radio and TV stations and newsrooms all my life. They believe that if they are out of step with you, if you feel a certain way, and their news is incongruent with you, then you're going to switch channels - they believe that you are looking for congruence, you're looking for things that are consistent with the way you feel.

What they also want to report is when the stock market's going down. They want to report bad news because they think that's the way you feel. If they're out of step with you, they're afraid you're gonna change the station. When the stock market's going down, it's just one bad negative story after another. When the stock market's going up, it's a lot of enlightening happy stories - because they want to be congruent.

There are always an infinite number of negative stories and an infinite number of positive stories. But you're not really getting a real report on what's happening; you're getting what they believe is going to make you want to listen to them longer. Right now, the media love to cover bad stories about COVID because they believe that that gets them high ratings. They believe that you tune in to negative stories about COVID, that you want to hear about the countries that aren't being vaccinated because they're too poor to get vaccinations.

The media reports about the vaccines side effects, how all the people in the U.S. get them, and the hospitals are filling up and blah, blah, blah. And they think that you want to hear this. And as you're hearing it, a lot of you actually believe it. And we can't talk about anything else because there's this distraction – like the negative stories about the fact that there are supply chain disruptions, that the manufacturers can't manufacture enough and everybody's short of inventory.

How can there be an inventory shortage? Well, they can't get anybody to drive the trucks. Why? Because the government's sending them all kinds of free money. I don't think it's that the truck drivers are afraid they're gonna get COVID inside their truck. I think it's that they've just got another source of money. And besides, some of the truck drivers that are hauling containers have to wait in line to get containers. And they have to wait in traffic, and you know, it's just not a good job anymore. So they go and work for FedEx or something. And one other thing… don't forget that production is down. The people that would otherwise be inventing new productive solutions, they're not doing that. They're too distracted, and they're worrying about COVID.

Why is this distraction going on? How distracted are we? How is it interfering with productivity? You certainly know that COVID isn't even close to being as lethal as the Spanish Flu was back in, I guess, 1912 or whatever. Most of the people that have gotten COVID don't even know they had it – they thought maybe it was a cold. The only people that have ever been in danger from COVID are old, or overweight, or have had a transplant, or have big problems with their immunity and their body's resistance.

So why, with all this opportunity I talk about, are people not able to make any money? Why are most people going to be left behind? Well, I'm here to see that you aren't one of the many who gets left behind. Maybe it's finally your turn. And I guess it's up to me to make sure that you get your turn. At least to make sure you get an equal spot at the starting line. Let me share a little story with you.

You're Inheriting a World Without Borders

You're Inheriting a World Without Borders

Your life as an investor is about to change forever. In fact, it's already changed. Your life as an investor, as a businessman or woman, your life as a member of humanity has changed in countless ways. And the changes are far more significant than the changes that came with the bicycle, the automobile, or radio and TV. In fact, the changes in your life from an economic standpoint are more profound than anything that's happened to humans in 500 years!

Before the printing press, only a select few could read and benefit from the developing information, the skills, the insights, and the opportunities that were sweeping the globe. The printing press allowed the transmission of radical new ideas in the fields of science, geography, and agriculture. Suddenly kings, queens, and nobles like Isabella, Elizabeth, Sir Walter Raleigh, and Columbus were becoming richer than anyone who had come before them.

World trade developed as these fortunate few figured out that we live on a spherical planet that circles the sun. They prospered far beyond their wildest dreams, sending ships around the world and conquering continents. They brought back tobacco, rubber, spices, tea, and gunpowder and sold it to their countrymen. They used the inventions of our Western civilization – transportation, information flow, science, and the art of modern warfare - to subdue the existing empires in all corners of the globe. In the process, they were able to accumulate most of the world's wealth, all for the benefit of that small European enclave that was the precursor of our civilization.

The seed of that revolution was planted with the development of the printing press, and it grew and developed for the next 500 years, culminating in the U.S. and the republic for which it stands. Since then, we've ruled the world. We've cured disease, shared ideas, and broadcasted drama, both real and imagined. We developed music, pictures, and sounds through motion pictures, then radio, then TV. We travelled to all corners of the Earth, to the moon, and then sent rockets around our solar system and our galaxy. And as humans advanced through the transmission of our culture, we Americans, the beneficiaries of all this progress, became ever richer and ever more powerful.

It was easy to believe we'd developed an everlasting monopoly. Think of it. We owned every new idea and every new invention. We won every war, dictated policy, and defeated all comers in every competition. We created the best universities and research facilities. We accumulated almost all the wealth, power, status, and all the comfort.

We'd built a better mousetrap, and they came. The very best and the very brightest came to the United States to study and to invent. And they stayed, building the most prosperous country that could ever have been conceived in this little corner of the galaxy.

To be sure, we put giant telescopes into orbit and learned to unravel the secrets of our universe going back billions of years. Can you conceive of just how long a couple of billion years is? It's the age of our planetary development, yet humans only learned to cultivate wheat 10,000 years ago. What a ride it's been as we developed communities, towns, cities, countries, and eventually alliances like Axis and NATO. So, what now? What's changed?

If you haven't noticed, the worldwide web has ushered in a new order. Everyone on the planet can now easily acquire the same information and the same education. In past centuries, only that tiny group of nobles could collaborate in ways now made possible for the entire world, all due to the new technologies. But now, inspired by our freedom, ingenuity, courage, and inventiveness, the rest of the world has learned our lessons. They've duplicated our cultural advances. And they're catching up.

To many of us it feels as though we're falling back, but we're not; they're simply moving ahead at electronic speed. Life in this new century is all about new fuels, new power, new forms of energy and automation. All over the world, people are now doing everything our most creative ancestors dreamed of over the last 10,000 years.

What's changed, you ask? Look around you. Today you, along with nearly eight billion other human beings, you woke up in a world without economic borders. We now know there are few limits on what our species can accomplish. We're taller and stronger; we run faster and live longer. And we enjoy comforts that even the nobility of the past could only dream of.

The borders are dissolving. There's no meaningful U.S. economy, no meaningful U.S. stock market. You're not limited to dollars, because you have access to every currency and every opportunity. You have access to eight billion new customers too, but you face fierce competition from eight billion relentless competitors. You may find the idea frightening or daunting, but you can't afford to pretend it's not happening, or you'll quickly be left behind. Billions of people are ready to sacrifice more and work harder than you are, because they're determined to give their families what you have.

But wait. We also have unprecedented advantages. We've been saving and accumulating surplus wealth for the past hundred years, while those new guys were still in the fields planting rice. They need our capital, and they're willing to pay premium prices for the opportunity to use it. We know exactly what they need and what they'll buy, and we've already been through all the steps they're about to take.

We can use our insights, our position, and our capital to finance the world's march forward, and allow those billions to work for us! We can help them win their battles and we can ride on their waves of success. Unfortunately, many of our fellow countrymen will opt instead to live in fear and denial. They'll hang on by their fingernails and squander their energy trying to hold the rest of the world back, to stifle the relentless advance of the human race as it catches up with us.

My mission for the years left of my life is to help you use your capital efficiently and skillfully. To help put Investor 1.0 to rest and facilitate the birth and development of Investor 2.0 - a new breed of investor, conscious and awake, who gets to take advantage of every new development and lead the human race to where it's inevitably headed anyway.

The best stock pickers, the most brilliant economists and financial thinkers join me daily on radio and TV; I meet with them socially, and we share business ideas. It's a joy for me because I get to process the best information on the planet and pass it on to you as quickly and as thoroughly as I possibly can. This book has proven to be very satisfying to me in that endeavor.

Of course, we won't ever be able to identify every opportunity. We'll never know whether we're missing something somewhere; in fact, I always assume we are. But we continue to march forward, always making progress, always stronger, always richer, keeping each other awake, and using our precious capital to help the billions around the world get what they want and need.

Join me and the thousands of others who are getting to ride on the success and progress of our world, a world of eight billion opportunities, eight billion competitors. From an economic standpoint, it's a new world. A world without borders.

What's First?

Throughout the course of this book, there will be times when I want to get very specific with you. We'll talk about various investment techniques, and those techniques are as valid today and tomorrow as they were yesterday. The investments themselves, however, well let's face it… we know that things are in constant change. I'm giving you my best ideas and strategies, although by the time you read this, some of them may have succeeded, played out, or even failed.

That's OK, because I'm giving you these ideas as an example of how you should be thinking. Take them in that spirit, because my mission is to help you transform yourself into the new species of think-for-yourself investor you'll have to be in this world without economic borders.

Our world is connected and networked as never before. We send our thoughts to each other everywhere and anywhere via e-mail, video conference, and streaming audio. We collaborate, we entertain each other, and we even finance each other across the borders.

That means the rest of the world is at our doorstep; so yes, we'll talk a lot about how you can take advantage of this new "globalized" economy. But make no mistake about it: For all intents and purposes, it is American ingenuity that created the wealth our neighbors want so desperately to share in. And there are plenty of great American companies to invest in - companies that stand as strong as the Rock of Gibraltar, companies that will continue to stand, continue to grow, continue to be some of the best investments available to make you rich, and richer.

As I am writing this, you and I still need and want and buy devices from the smartest American companies whose stock in trade is Artificial Intelligence

– the key to the future. You are joining us in the business of devices and ideas that are bargains to us, and extremely profitable to the companies that invented them.

I have little doubt that I'll be buying and selling their stocks for the rest of my life. I've come to understand the companies and the pricing of their stocks, and that will also be your job for the rest of your economic life. It only takes a little experience and practice. You'll get it, just as you learned to throw a football or play ping pong, to shoot pool or draw blueprints, or to sing or dance.

I'll also be watching (and buying and selling) the Blackstone Group. I'll talk about this brilliant company and just a few others in more detail later, but for now, just imagine how Blackstone can fit into your life. Smart people continue to invest billions into Blackstone, and with its experience and savvy, Blackstone uses that money to buy companies, take them private, then develop and sell them, usually for a huge profit. I'm sure I'll buy and sell Blackstone many times over the course of the rest of my life. Again, you can easily learn to do the same thing, and this is a perfect company for the billionaire acquisition techniques we've been talking about throughout this book.

The point to be made here is that this is not just us and them. It's all of us; it's a network. A worldwide network to be sure, but hey, it takes a phone connection or a computer connection the same amount of time to go around the globe as it does to go around the corner, and that's why Blackstone is dominating worldwide.

As an American, you're privileged to belong to a culture made up of inventors and innovators, a vast group of people who have been able not only to survive, but to thrive on their spirit of adventure and a vast store of knowledge, all long before our neighbors around the world began to "catch on." If you're ready to join in, good. Now, let's see how we ever got into this terrific position in the first place.

Why America Has Always Dominated (Part 1)

This is going to be the era when we Americans, who have until now, been the inspiration to the whole world, get to watch the ascent of everybody else, while we do our best to fritter away our power and wealth.

The truth is if we keep ignoring the free spirit and willingness to take a chance and assume the risk of losing what got us to where we are, we will see some decline. Much of this book is about how to think globally and share in the good fortune of those around the world that we have inspired. More than that, it's about how you can join in and get rich helping them get what we have - that which they are determined to get!

But don't be fooled. The real long-term success of the United States is still ahead of us. At the moment we may be slowing our own development by focusing on how we split the pie, rather than how we grow the pie, but life in this great country is cyclical. That's a very important point which we'll discuss at length.

Our society still has more freedom than any other on this planet, and when the government's policies don't work out, we're better able to change policies and governments than anyone else.

That's exactly what will happen, eventually. So, for now, you and I will make lots of money acknowledging that foolish U.S. policies are going to set us back a little as a country and give others with courage and initiative a chance to catch up and even surpass us in certain areas - for a little while.

Through that whole medium-term plan, don't forget for one minute that the worst bet ever conceived on planet Earth has been a bet against American ingenuity, the American economy, and American power. History is littered with the limp bodies of those deceased, and the shells that remain of those still alive, who have made that bet against the United States - from Hitler and Tojo, to Khrushchev and Brezhnev, Osama Bin laden and alBaghdadi. I, for one do not plan to join them.

There are major reasons for our success. Our advantages over other nations are so profound they're difficult to overcome. Sometimes they lead us to make mistakes rooted in overconfidence and hubris, but we've always recovered, and when the whole world gets used to selling America, I can assure you, I will be buying.

The best and the brightest came to America, because they saw the big magic "O" -opportunity. And what created that opportunity was the very nature of the place itself. The guys who landed here way back when, landed in one of the most fertile, well-developed places on the face of the planet.

It's a well-designed place with better resources and a better setup than anywhere else in the world. From sea to shining sea, we have good, arable land. Easy to grow stuff on, it's the largest piece of contiguous arable land in the entire world. The middle of the country is made up of prairie land that's perfect for crops; it didn't even need to be cleaned up before farming. And there's more very good farmland on the East Coast, the West Coast, and down South.

There's good, arable land elsewhere in the world, but it's mixed in with mountains and jungles and deserts. We've never been saddled with the enormous burden of having to focus all our energy on trying to feed a country full of hungry, undernourished people, because it's never been hard for us to get large tracts of land set up to feed our population. Most other nations spend all their time and energy just trying to get food. The next reason is travel. How easy is this? We have a couple of mountain ranges a few thousand miles apart, but other than that, it's flat! We've easily built roads for horses and stagecoaches and buggies, roads for cars and trucks. We've easily built railroads north, south, east, and west. To build roads in most other countries, you've got to blast through mountains, or dig your way through treacherous land, or clear your way through jungles, and so on. It's slow, tedious, and very expensive work. And I'm talking about everybody: Europe, Asia, South America, Africa, China, Russia, all of them. They have tiny little pieces of arable land mixed with very, very rough terrain, where it's extremely difficult to move people around.

Those other countries need gigantic armies, too. Because of the layout of the land, armies need to be stationed all over the place in every key populated area. We've survived throughout the ages with smaller armies because it's so easy to move them around. These things are all important because the more resources you have the more creative you can be. We started writing music and developing the arts while many countries were still trying to figure out how to build roads. And don't even get me started on the rivers and waterways in this country. Not only is the land fertile, but we've also got rivers that traverse the country in every imaginable direction.

Now Europe has a lot of rivers, but they all move in one direction without connecting. Here, the rivers connect! And it's so incredibly easy to use that network of rivers to move everything around. It's made it easy to develop cities, easy to get food there, easy to get equipment to the farms and to the armies.

America is also blessed with great jagged coastlines, which make for great ports. It's easy for us to bring in big ships. They can anchor in those deep-water bays just offshore and load their goods. In many of them they can dock right at the port city, which means easy connections to the rivers and easy means of transporting people and goods. How could this not have turned out to be the dominant force in our world? It's really a great place to live and develop a population of people. We very easily accomplish things that are, for other nations, a considerable challenge. And that's just the beginning.

Why America Has Always Dominated (Part Two)

Because of the physical nature of the United States, as described earlier, it was relatively easy to develop this country. And because that in and of itself created opportunities, it lent itself to an immigration of very intelligent, inventive, and creative people. They were attracted by this wonderful, fertile environment. And once they got here, they began to innovate, which only caused the advantages and opportunities to increase. It's what would happen in the NFL if the best team got to pick first in the draft. Imagine what kind of a team they'd build in a very short time!

I want to give credit to my good friend Harry Dent for this next line of thinking, and I'm compelled to include it because it really helps define the makeup of the generations of people who carry this country ever forward. Harry called one of them the "Bob Hope generation," and it had a particular role to play. You see, the generation that preceded it was the Henry Ford generation. They were very innovative, building and discovering new things, new technologies, the assembly line, and all the great inventions that served as the building blocks for many of the things that we use today.

The Bob Hope generation fought World War II and made it safe to live here. And it was Harry Dent, who pointed out that these generations alternate. One generation invents and innovates; the next distributes and takes the innovation to the masses. One generation built the assembly line for cars, the next created gigantic car companies.

Then came the Baby Boomers to start the innovation process all over again. It goes without saying that computers, along with an incredibly high-speed Internet, have been the greatest of those achievements and contributions. Next? Maybe it will be a generation that will have computers that work without I.T. guys. Eventually, we'll have a generation of computers that work so well and are so easy to manage that we'll be choosing them by how well they go with our decor, as we do with lamps and telephones.

So here are all these very smart, very innovative folks in a land where opportunities abound, and there's another new and exciting one waiting around every corner. They take advantage of every one of these opportunities and are now inventing new ways to do things; one in particular is augmenting the human brain with computer networking and wireless digital communication devices. Together these elements facilitate the transmission of information at a speed past generations could not have even imagined.

All this led us to accelerate the speed at which more new innovations could occur. Suddenly our scientists can map the gene, and they can go back 15 billion years and look at things through the use of space telescopes and computer modeling. They're no longer limited to the use of their own brains. Every American benefits from the fantastic new ways to communicate with each other. Just like the rivers found in this country allowed a faster means of delivering goods and messages, the rivers of communication now flow at a speed never conceived before.

Naturally, as the resources increased and improved, more folks wanted to join in on the fun. The Baby Boomers were the first ones fortunate enough to reap the benefits of all those improvements in communication and manufacturing and so forth. This was a large generation of people. There were a lot of them - strong, bright, and innovative. So you can see how things grew exponentially.

I guess the final word on this country's ability to dominate is this: many of those other countries and their societies, particularly the Europeans, are traditionally noblemen with deep heritages. They're steeped in their owned strata, and they're basically stuck there.

The folks who came over to America, however, were adventurous, ambitious middle-class people. They were merchants who were traveling, trying to develop more trade. Kings and queens and barons and baronesses don't care much about getting out there and developing trade. I guess they're too busy looking at their art. The merchants I spoke of (the middle-class folks) weren't so steeped in their traditions. They were far too busy, out there looking for new and exciting ways to conquer new frontiers and always seeking new adventures. You might say they were the artists, not the art collectors.

Why Things Are Changing

That's a lot of great news. Too good to continue this way forever? Well, let me say this; this generation I've been talking about, these energetic innovators, have aged out and been replaced by a new generation who has brought with it a digital transformation more significant than the printing press, radio and TV and ideas we haven't even heard of today. And once the key to progress became technology (instead of rivers), the transfer of knowledge has taken over the world.

Compare the gifts of America with our new adversary, China. Now, there's a place with little arable land, poor roads, and few rivers. So, why all the fuss about China? We Americans have so transformed the world that the new highway of knowledge is the Internet, and China and the rest of the world are using that technology to try to beat us at our own game.

Rich and mature, many of us tend to sit around thinking that we have all the advantages, and no one could possibly have a shot at catching up with us. We forget that as we've prospered, we've taught them the game so well that they might become better at the game than we are. Our realization of this fact has been very slow in coming, but it will become clear quickly and suddenly. This book is not about fighting the inevitable; it's about loving it, embracing it, and riding that wave.

The problem for the average wealth of Americans in the near term is the fact that Americans just don't seem to get it. We're not getting the fact that when you print trillions of dollars (that's what we're doing, you know), you weaken yourself. Other people in the world are beginning to compete. If we come to understand that you can't make laws dictating that folks buy cars they don't like, then those folks are going to go out and buy cars that are made elsewhere. We don't seem to understand that when people get fed up and feel too much pressure, they can just up and move their businesses elsewhere.

We also don't seem to get it that you can't reward people for being lazy and slothful and get the same level of ingenuity and aggression we've become used to over the last couple of hundred years. You can't punish people for being risk takers because those people are going to either stop being innovative risk takers and/or they're going to go somewhere else and conduct business. We (and I say that collectively) don't seem to understand this stuff. How did we get to this point? How did this all happen? Let me see if I can explain it to you.

The people running just about all the countries in the world have all been educated in the same places. They've all been attending our Ivy League schools, or Stanford or NYU or USC or the University of Chicago. The Chinese, the Pakistanis, the Japanese - the people running all the countries around the world - they were educated in the same universities in America as were many of our own leaders.

Here's the difference. The people running those countries majored in economics and finance. The people running our country studied political science and law. That's the reason they get it and we don't. That may be a bit metaphorical, and a bit oversimplified, but the bottom line is that's why they get it and we don't. There are other reasons, too.

Take for instance the idea that there have always been communists and socialists - and by the way, the idea of communism is not in and of itself evil. The idea basically says, "Look, let's make things equal and spread the wealth, and make things fair for everybody." The only reason that idea has been fading instead of growing and proliferating, is because it hasn't really worked that well. You've seen it; these guys get into power and make bad decisions and then typically become selfish and corrupt. The idea of spreading the wealth isn't a bad idea; it just doesn't work so well. The places where there have been incentives have generally become more productive, that's all.

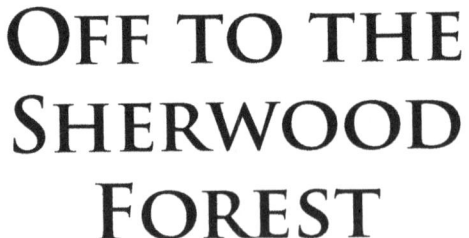

OFF TO THE SHERWOOD FOREST

Off to the Sherwood Forest

Look, it's a nice idea. It would be lovely if we could all share and everybody could be equal and happy. My good friend and partner Arthur Laffer has a great story, and I've told it often and sometimes forget to give him credit, so this is Arthur's take on a classic tale, ok? It's the one about Robin Hood and his band of merry men. It's a wonderful, romantic story.

Robin Hood is in Sherwood Forest, he's got his green tights on, he's taking from the rich and giving it all to the poor; it's lovely, and he's a lovely guy. He gets the girl too, Maid Marian, and it's terrific. And that's what some of our politicians would love to do. (No, not get the girl - that's another book.) They want to spread the wealth, just like Robin. But there's a problem.

How many times do you think those rich noblemen will keep going back through Sherwood Forest once they know Robin Hood is out there? See, that's the problem with this story. They rich guys stop coming! They've wised up to being robbed every time they go into Sherwood, so they quit going there!

The point is you can make the rules any way you want to, but if I can, through some technological advance, go anywhere I want to, I'm going. If I can use email or whatever to move my entire think-tank to Dubai in a split second, I'm out of here. But some of our politicians just don't get that. They don't get the idea that I've discovered that Robin Hood is laying in wait for me in Sherwood Forest, and so I have wisely found another route. What I don't get is that they don't get it.

Here's another contributing factor that is equally dramatic: a 24-hour cycle of streaming TV, and non-stop news and information. I participate in it, I love being a part of it, and if it's up to me, I'll never stop being part of it.

The people who run the media have figured out how to make it interesting and entertaining. They've got beautiful people in beautiful make-up with beautiful smiles and great clothes. So now, you've got millions and millions of people all over the world watching 24-hour news. And it's not just the super-intelligent; everybody is watching, because like I said it's all so entertaining. But look what's happened here in the United States.

These past few elections are the first time in history that an election has been determined by people who understand block voting, they understand the primaries, they understand everything about the election and the voting and the counting processes; they even understand the red states and the blue states, because they've studied the processes over and over.

They've seen it presented like some sporting event on TV, but guess what? They never studied the history of western civilization, they never studied economics, they never studied literature, and they don't know what they're voting for, or who they're voting for, or what he or she stands for.

What's worse, they don't understand the impact of the things that they've said yes to -things that have been tried, but don't work. They don't know this stuff. They think they're going to be able to tax these rich guys, they think they're going to be able to force people to buy union-made cars from Detroit; they think all these things will happen, but they won't. And the reason, as my friend Arthur Laffer so eloquently stated when he gave me his spin on the story of Robin Hood, is that these folks will simply go somewhere else, where life (and doing business) is just not so hard or expensive.

To Review

Indeed, America won the lottery when it came to being the ideal place to create an ideal land of milk and honey. Everything came together. The best and brightest came here. Individualism flourished. There were plenty of resources, plenty of space. We built our roads and railroads, and the Bob Hope generation liberated the world, first by winning World War II and then by mass producing some of the greatest innovations created by humanity. Our baby boom generation followed by inventing a whole new technology. Technology helped augment the human brain and solve virtually all our problems, or so it seemed.

We now know that resources in the ground are fixed; either you have them, or you don't. But with the aid of technology, ideas can now be duplicated anywhere. Inventiveness can spread anywhere. People used to come to the United States and learn, and then stay here and build their lives. Now they come here and learn, then go back home to do their inventing and innovating.

As a nation, we're less inventive, less adventurous, and as a nation where the predominant generation is getting older, we're less militaristic. We prefer a defense to an offense. And generally speaking, as a nation we are not as hungry as we once were. By nature of the fact that you're reading this book, I can only surmise that you're working toward excluding yourself from that group. Well-done, Investor 2.0.

So how do we do this? We emerge from the fog of denial that has us trying to replay the 1990s. We stop feeling threatened by innovative, smart, hard-working people around the world who are determined to work harder than we do. We use our capital to develop natural resources to feed their growth, as billions of them move from the country to the city, following our model to build their societies. The success of technology companies in the 1990s attracted so much capital and created so much capacity in those areas that profits were cut and monopolies were lost, thereby making those very areas less fruitful for investors. Some of those businesses will be fine, but to get my investment dollar today, a company must have a brilliant Asia strategy, no matter where in the world it resides.

You and I will be able to make big money, easily and without that much creativity, by financing the finding, processing, storing and transporting of the building blocks of society - the things you absolutely have to have to move billions of people from the country to the city.

Those billions of determined American-lifestyle-wanna-bees, will need every bit of copper, zinc, cement, platinum, titanium, iron, steel, coal, oil, and pure drinking water that they can lay their hands on, and we've got the resources to help supply them. These kinds of investments are now easy to make. I'll be naming many of the ones I'm committing my money to, and I'll explain strategies you may have never seen or heard before. They're strategies the very rich have had access to for a long time.

You've always had access to everything you'll learn in this book; I've simply compiled it for you, which will at the very least save you a trip to the library. Face it, nobody goes to the library anymore (and we'll talk about that a little later, too). At any rate, armed with this information, using your capital to finance this most powerful and unstoppable movement in the history of the human race should be a no-brainer.

How could you not want to own a company that provides inexpensive online education in English to the Chinese, to teach technology skills, and whatever else they need to know to bring hundreds of millions of them into the middle class? How could you not want a piece of a government-owned real estate broker in a country that's preparing to move a group of people equal to the entire population of the United States into new cities? How could you not?

We've had some building booms in the United States, and many of us have made some pretty good money participating in them. But close your eyes and consider this: in the coming years the Chinese are going to build - from the ground up - the combined equivalent of New York City, Los Angeles, Chicago, Atlanta, Miami, Phoenix, Houston, Dallas, Fort Worth, Denver, and San Francisco. Where in the world are we, the citizens of this economically borderless planet, ever going to find, mine, and produce enough raw materials to do all that? How are we going to store it or transport it all?

I'll tell you. We're going to need a lot of help. The people in China are going to have to get labor and materials from Australia, Indonesia, South Korea, and Taiwan, as well as South America and Africa. Just think for a minute about how much capital Europeans and Americans used and how much wealth we created building out projects like that over a period of 200 years. And now, think how rich those will be who are instrumental in helping all this happen, when the development is compressed into just a couple of decades! Throughout this book I'll continue to talk about how you and I are going to provide financing for all this.

As you're reading, keep this picture in your mind. Keep reminding yourself about how those of us who finance this large social movement are going to make more money than anyone has ever made on this planet before. Think about how much money is going to be made just helping these billions of new middle-class citizens of our borderless world get pure drinking water.

You and I already know exactly what these billions are going to be buying, and we already know how to help them get what they're totally determined to get. There's no doubt they will succeed, so who wouldn't want to help them get there, and be paid very handsomely for doing so?

Welcome to the New World, Investor 2.0

Now, here's a crucial admonition. I don't know anything about you. Some things that are great investments and projects for me may not be right for you. You may have special tax, personal, and other factors that I know nothing about. As the most up-to-date, smartest, upgraded investor, you must get into the habit of evaluating ideas instead of just finding people you can trust to lead you. I'll talk about that a lot, but take this reminder seriously, right here and right now.

Think through the ideas I give you. Don't just go out and commit money to things I'm investing in without taking the responsibility of knowing exactly what you're doing. This book is to entertain you, and to condition your mind to take advantage of the huge opportunity that is now open to you. Take my work as a place to start the research, to support your evolution into a whole new life form, a new species of investor, a conscious investor who is free of denial, and who actually invests for profit instead of self-esteem.

At the very top of the food chain, right now, all the players know that power is synonymous with responsibility. I can promise you with absolute certainty that you will begin to attract great wealth the minute you decide to be totally responsible for your every thought and action. My life, my happiness, and my wealth are not determined by the President, by Goldman Sachs, The Fed, The Hedge Funds, The Chinese, or CNBC. You can be equally free, equally powerful, and you can start getting richer, right now.

From this moment forward, take responsibility for every single thing you decide to commit your money to. You have all the time and all the opportunities you could ever need.

The very richest people in the world all know this: your money belongs in your pocket unless you have something compelling to commit to. The very rich don't feel pressure to hurry up and invest. They know the resource that is most scarce and in most demand is money. They have it, and everyone else needs it. That means they can be very choosy about where they commit. And when they do commit, they do it with maximum power, and use all the tools you are learning about in this book.

You can do the same; you can learn to think like a rich person in a world of infinite opportunity, a world without economic borders. And starting right now, today, you're well on your way. Now then, let's see what challenges you're facing.

WALL ST. LIES - LIAR, LIAR STARTS THE FIRE!

Wall St. Lies - Liar, Liar Starts the Fire!

It wasn't too many years ago that I did a project called Wall Street Lies. It was a package of audio CDs that I put together because there was a story to be told. A lot of it was about the right and wrong of what was going on at the time with many of the brokerage firms, insurance companies, and other people who were selling financial products.

Wall Street Lies was my means of pointing out the myths, the facts, and most importantly, the lies you'd hear every day… on radio or TV, on the street, from your neighbors (most of whom didn't know any better), and in many cases from your "advisor."

One of the many things these guys would tell you is that, although what you do matters considerably, when you do it isn't really all that important. Most of them, then and now, would have you believe that timing the market is impossible anyway, so why lie awake at night trying to figure out how to do something that can't be done? "You can't time the market" remains one of the biggest of all the Wall Street lies.

If you've lost lots of money on good companies that have been successful, or will at least at times be successful, you already know what a foolish idea that is. The truth is you'd better time the markets. I for one am doing my best to seek good timing in everything I do during my remaining days on this planet.

Diversification: There's another lie. Those so-called experts would also suggest that you rely on diversification to keep you safe. This means just invest in a little of everything, instead of choosing the place to use your financial power. I don't think that idea ever made sense, but when the entire market was on the rise and everything was going up together, it made a good story, and it justified assuming risk without knowing exactly what you were doing.

Presumably that also made it alright to rely on advice from people who didn't know much about investing. You probably don't need an exposé on that idea at this point, because so much money has recently been lost by good, intelligent people who were lulled into believing they were safe. They figured that by being diversified they didn't have to be aware of the world changing around them.

But the world has changed gradually and imperceptibly each day. We reached a tipping point, and all the markers for carelessness, arrogance, hubris, excessive risk and insensitivity to timing came due at the same time. It was as if suddenly someone shouted "FIRE!" on a crowded planet and everyone in the world ran for the exits at the same time, catching most investors completely off guard - and doing away with decades of savings.

The point is this: Today you woke up in a world without economic borders. That world will grow at four, five, or even six percent for the foreseeable future. For the most part, the growth around the world will support real economic development in countries we never thought of back in the 1990s. Great American companies, smart American investors, and powerful American financial institutions will feed, finance, and help create the steady forward march of civilization around the world.

Rah, Rah, Rah! MatchBook U! (Formulas)

Again, they think we're stupid and they treat us that way. These salesmen have no idea how to make money. If they did, they would have some and they wouldn't be spending their lives in little cubicles, but I digress. The point here is that your goal is to MAKE MONEY. To change your life. You aren't going to do this according to a formula that everyone else is following also. That's how you play defense. We're here to score.

We don't believe we can change our lives by following the same formula millions of others follow. We have to apply courage, brains and ingenuity to make a difference in the world. Obviously, there is no formula for doing that. Here's an example of a formula that will keep you poor, if you follow it, and yet millions do – without thinking. It was especially designed for old people, and they teach it at Matchbook U.

Now for those of you who've never heard of Matchbook U, it's that school full of courses that some wishful thinkers take instead of learning and mastering their subject. (It's advertised a lot on the back of matchbook covers). They want to get away easy, and they succeed in accomplishing very little.

But about this formula: it says that old people should take the number 100, subtract their age, and then the result is the percentage of their money that should be in stocks, and the rest should be in bonds. In other words, if a person is 80 years old, he should have twenty percent of his money in stocks and eighty percent of it in bonds; 50 years old, he should be half in stocks, half in bonds, and so on.

I'm convinced that this old formula was designed by 40-year-olds making $40,000 a year who have no idea of what old people need. Anytime I've encountered an 80-year-old and offered a suggestion about what they should buy… well, the really smart ones look at me and say, "I want to know what you're buying."

I think the guys who design this type of plan think they're catering to an elderly person's concern about when they might die, and their natural fear of growing less competent.

I simply advise these folks that the real problems come if they continue to live! Usually, we have a good chuckle over that point and then talk some good common sense. That's what old people really like anyway—good, common sense.

A very amusing irony (well, it would be amusing if it weren't so harmful) is the fact that these guys are still seeing bonds as the safe place to hide money. If they had any understanding of economics at all, they would realize that bonds lose money in a world of rising interest rates and rising inflation.

The pathetic attempt to be safe by hiding your money in the most dangerous possible place is just classic ignorance and incompetence. Unfortunately, their training is not about making money. It is about selling the products their employers tell them to sell.

So these stockbrokers and these insurance salesmen, any of these guys who'd want to sell you some kind of financial product on behalf of some company or institution, they had come to refer to themselves as financial consultants, or planners, or advisors. I'll give you the real definition of those terms later, but implicit in these words is the idea that these guys are hired by you and paid by you, and that their responsibility is to do what's best for the guy paying them. That of course would be you!

It's another lie. In fact, nothing could be further from the truth. An insurance guy is a selling agent, and he doesn't work for you. He works for the insurance company, which has a particular agenda - they want to sell their products. And your stockbroker? He's not a registered investment advisor. He's not obligated to act on your behalf any more than a real estate broker is obligated to act on behalf of the buyer. On the contrary, he acts on behalf of the seller.

Don't misunderstand me. I'm not saying your buddy is a bad guy. I'm saying that you may think he's going to be right there for you and that he knows how to make money. But there's no evidence of that; in fact, in most cases, he's probably not even making a lot of money himself. Go ahead. Look out in the driveway - what kind of car is he driving?

Listen, the important thing to know is that these guys went to some place that showed them how to magnify the need for insurance and front-end loaded products, and the story they tell you is the same one they tell all their clients.

They'd hand you a laundry list of financial products: "Here! Take a look at this list, and don't worry about whether it's a good time to buy because everybody knows there's no better time than the present. And since you don't have a clue about what to buy or when to sell this stuff anyway, well, heck, you might as well buy it all from me right now, right?"

Wait; hold on, there's more.

Let me give you an example of how a typical financial planning meeting might go with one of these Matchbook U grads; maybe you've been through this one before. Let's say you're married, and you're the breadwinner for your family. Let's say you're 40 years old with two kids. So, this guy comes out and takes the information from you and then feeds it into his computer. It comes back with a story about how much insurance you don't have and, of course, what you really should have.

So, the computer says you need this much insurance because God forbid, if you were to die, your spouse would have this much of an income shortage. Note that his computer assumes that even though you're only 40 years old when you die, your spouse will do nothing but sit around and watch TV for the rest of his/her life and be totally dependent on your life insurance policy. Did you ever think about that?

"And besides," he says, "your spouse isn't going to help people around the world get what they want. That nest egg you're trying to create is not going to help finance the greatest social movement in history." My friend, if you're listening to this guy, you're being duped. You're being told that timing is unnecessary, and that appropriate action is not achievable.

And the worst of it is that this kind of thinking causes you to commit huge amounts of your capital in the wrong place, and in fact it assures that your spouse is going to need a huge infusion of cash. It also assumes that once your lonely widow or widower gets that cash infusion, they'll continue to be totally ignorant of the greatest transformation in the history of the human race. I hope you get this. Otherwise, you're going to need all that insurance.

Hey, what if the computer assumes you'll only be disabled? Nope, sorry, the answer is still essentially the same. The assumption is that no matter what bad thing happens to you, your family will just sit in front of the TV for the rest of their lives, and must be supported without digging into the principal of the insurance policy. In other words, as the breadwinner, you have to have enough insurance so that the income from the insurance pays for every expense the family incurs ever again, even if you die at age 40!

OK, I'll stop there. This book isn't about insurance anyway, right? What I'm addressing is the people who would come out and sell you a cornucopia of financial products using those silly arguments cited above and posing as financial planners. Now that we've done that, I assume you realize that the insurance policy our 40-year-old friend almost bought wouldn't have been his best move. Let's talk about some alternatives.

Good Old Matchbook U - The Faculty, Staff, and Graduates

This takes us back to the subject of what that insurance salesman (and guys like him) have sold the American public. They've sold you a bill of goods that has, in the final analysis, cost them their own jobs. All right then, who are these people anyway; are they experts? I'll let you be the judge, but let's analyze it. First of all, how do they get trained? Well, some go to real schools and get real finance degrees, but generally those guys end up working in a big building somewhere over in the investment-banking department doing the big money deals.

Now, the salespeople - the stockbrokers you get to talk to - they don't usually have that kind of education. They're more likely to have a bachelor's degree in - well, in something. Who knows, maybe finance, maybe economics, maybe accounting, whatever. And then they get sent to (that's right), good old Matchbook U. You know, the alma mater of those guys we talked about earlier - the guys who graduate from those courses you see advertised on matchbook covers who then go on to be salespeople.

These stockbrokers and salespeople are, if not coerced, certainly encouraged to get that education. When you go to a financial planner it's with the idea of making more money, of having an improvement in your bottom line, but these guys don't learn techniques to make more money; they only learn how to execute what we laughingly call Modern Portfolio Theory. It's what they believe to be the skill of engaging in an arbitrage strategy.

That's the simultaneous buying and selling of the same negotiable financial instruments or commodities in different markets in order to make an immediate profit without risk. And to allocate assets that garner a risk-free profit, a profit based on purposely choosing to have your actions relate to something other than the real world or to the times in which you live. More precisely, it's their lack of skill to engage in arbitrage.

What they're trying to accomplish with their Modern Portfolio Theory is to convince you that there's nothing to know and that timing doesn't help - that in fact, timing doesn't really matter at all. The theory these guys work on is getting you to buy a little bit of everything, presumably so that you can only be a little bit wrong all the time.

Oh, and it's important that you understand this: these guys that you think of as brokers or salesmen are actually called "registered representatives" of a FINRA firm, of a brokerage firm or a broker-dealer. (A broker-dealer means that they are either the middleman in a transaction or they sell you stuff from their inventory, which would make them a dealer.) So, the company is actually called a broker-dealer, and your salesman-guide-advisor is actually called a registered representative. What's funny - well, actually it's not really funny - is that he or she is not permitted to originate any advice.

Don't misunderstand: Many of them will make it seem as though they are giving you advice. But let me say it again: They are not permitted to give advice; they're simply there to pass on the position of their firm. It involves quite a mess of bureaucratic technicalities, but it would probably help you to know the story of the SEC regulation of advisors versus what used to be the NASD (and is now called FINRA) and its regulation of broker- dealers and their registered representatives.

You see, a registered investment advisor is regulated by the SEC. He or she has an obligation to act in a fiduciary manner—that is, to act on behalf of and for the benefit of the client and give advice when he's acting in the capacity of an advisor. Yes, there are conflicts of interest, which are permissible; they simply must be disclosed.

Now, a broker is the actual sales company. Generally speaking, they're representing not the investor, but the company that needs to raise the money. So they owe fair treatment, yes, but there's not a fiduciary responsibility to advise - and I'm talking in particular now about your registered representative or salesman. His obligation is to act on behalf of his broker-dealer, who is in the business of raising money for the company who wants you to invest in them.

You need to understand that it's not possible to serve both masters, because what is defined as a good deal for the investor must then be a concession by the target company that the investor is investing in. Said another way, if it's a great deal for the company, then it's not such a great deal for the investor.

Imagine a conversation in which the broker-dealer goes to the big company, let's say IBM (or anybody really), and he says, "Well, interest rates are very low right now and there's a very big risk spread, so a company like yours which is very well known and obviously solvent, is gonna be able to get a very low interest rate right now. And so, I recommend that you go out and float a bond issue." Again, obviously, if it's good for the company trying to raise the money, it can't be good for the person who lends the money at a low interest rate. That makes sense, right?

Now, back to the story about the advisory and its requirements to disclose. Some years back the brokerage firms found that a lot of people were concerned about conflicts of interest. This happened around the end of the '90s when it became obvious that there were tremendous conflicts of interest and the brokerage firms weren't handling them very fairly. People started to think (and say) that they would rather have an advisor who had a fiduciary responsibility to the investor, that they would be able to trust them better. I think the public was right at that time.

But the brokerage firms came up with the idea— and by the way Merrill Lynch was in the forefront of this—they added the word "advisor" to their name and created what they called wrap accounts, accounts which made them look like an advisor. So now they have a new name, and instead of paying them individual commissions per transaction, you'd pay them a fixed amount per year. This, by the way, would typically add up to a little more than you'd otherwise pay in commissions.

So now the brokerage firm looks like a registered investment advisor. The difference being that the registered investment advisor owes that fiduciary advice. The brokerage firm makes commissions by raising money for the company that you invest in (rather than representing you, the investor). It's important that you understand that distinction.

Using the word advisor was deemed to be deceptive; it would make the brokerage firm look like a registered investment advisor and give the investor the impression that they're acting as his fiduciary. So, the position of the brokerage firms' industry was that they should get a special dispensation to use the word "advisor," but under SEC rules, if you use the word advisor you must disclose any conflicts of interest.

See, if you're a registered advisor, people are naturally trusting that you're their fiduciary. Moreover, the brokerage firms were not only seeking SEC permission to use the word, but special dispensation to avoid disclosure of their conflicts of interest! I hope this gives you some insight into the relationship and the difference between the two. The easiest way to remember this is when you hear the word advisor, beware. (Whew!)

Now then, where was I? Oh, yes, finally we've come to the heart of the matter, and here it is. Is the brokerage firm you're about to do business with a company of experts? Could you trust them even if they wanted to give you good advice? And what about that sales guy, the broker or registered representative, even if he really wants to give you good advice, is he an expert?

First, let's address the companies. You have to remember that now, as we look back on everything that's happened over the last 20 years, you can see that the scandal at the end of the '90s was all about the brokerage firms. Their analysts were actually out there touting stocks, and it later came to light that they were simultaneously sending e-mails and literally laughing about some of the recommendations they'd made.

They were obviously not following the advice that they were giving other people; they were making a mockery of their own business dealings. Here's where it gets interesting. Later, in fact just a few years ago, they actually began to follow their own trading advice. And when they did, they put themselves out of business in just one cycle! They're now owned by companies that had to get government money to bail them out because they followed their own advice too!

The biggest broker, the one that was in the forefront trying to use the word advisor without disclosing its conflict of interest, was actually bought by a bailed-out bank. Then, at the last minute (you may remember the scandal), Bank of America wanted to back out, but the government forced the CEO to buy the brokerage firm - which of course proceeded to pay itself huge bonuses with money that was earmarked for bailing out the business! Those, my friends, are the companies we're talking about.

Now how about the brokers themselves? They were trained by their brokerage firm, which understands all the brokers' capabilities and training perfectly, right? We presume the company understands the abilities of the salesman or registered representative. They educated this guy, they understand his skill set; they're paying him money because of his purported expertise, right? Right?

All right then, so let me ask this very simple question: How often do you think they ask him for advice about what they should do with their portfolio? How about their bond portfolio in particular? Now you have to ask yourself what it is that they want to sell you. And then ask yourself if this is the guy you want to buy anything from. Anything!

There are a lot of big ones, but I want to cover what might be the biggest Wall Street lie of all. It started out as a lie that the big brokers were foisting on the population. By now you know the big guys of whom I speak: Goldman Sachs, Morgan Stanley, Merrill Lynch and those kinds of guys. But what's happened is that over the last thirty years, these lies have become ubiquitous - they're everywhere.

And they've told them so much and so often that even the people who repeat them on television, like the analysts and reporters, they themselves start to believe them. And the people who want to be your financial advisor, or your broker, or your insurance agent – they're all trained to believe all these lies. It's been going on for many years and now they're passing these lies on to you.

And here it comes... and every financial expert will tell you this. Stick to investing in what you know! And it's all baloney. The lie is, "you're too dumb to actually do what we do. We here at (Goldman Sachs, Merrill Lynch, whoever), we're making a fortune investing money because we've got these brilliant MBAs, and they're sitting there with a bank of computers, and they're doing intensive original research all day".

What do you think would happen if I asked one of those guys... let's say I was his boss, and I said, "What are you doing today"? And he said, "Well, I'm investing in what I know".

The lie started with a great investment manager, Peter Lynch at Fidelity Magellan, who back in the 1970's attributed his success to investing in what he knew. The fact is, his fund was full of all kinds of companies in all kinds of industries, and if he was really an expert on all of them, he was a lot smarter than I am. Lynch was a great stock picker and a genius, and I'm sure his technique works for geniuses in general.

But consider this: If investing in things you know actually worked, you'd already be rich, wouldn't you?

It's pretty likely that the things you know haven't made you rich yet. And more importantly, do you think that Goldman Sachs, up at the top of the Empire State Building or wherever their top guys are - they make billions investing their money - do you think they stick with investing in things they know? Or do you think what they do is find out what people want and need and the companies that provide it, and learn all about them before investing in them?

They seek out companies that are making a profit, that can raise money easily, that have patents that are difficult to duplicate, that are difficult to compete with, companies that are leaders in their industry that are inventing great new ways to do things, and that are doing it profitably. An example of that would be CrowdStrike, a company that solves issues of hacking with artificial intelligence, and they do it for big companies. And for big money.

When we had that hacking going on in 2021 at the hands of those businessmen in Russia, they couldn't get through to any of the CrowdStrike clients. The minute they hit those clients, CrowdStrike's artificial intelligence figured them out, making those clients immune. And now they've developed a network for all their clients, the solution has spread throughout this network, and none of their clients, none of their customers, are vulnerable. And of course, we have to get past hacking in order to have the digital transformation that we want.

So this is a company that's the best at what they do, and each transaction is profitable. They keep creating new services and selling them to their customers. It's a great company. You may not know anything about it, but you better learn about it.

Goldman Sachs and Morgan Stanley made a fortune by investing in CrowdStrike and buying long term options on the stock. And we just made about thirty times our money over the last year by investing in it.

So the lie is, telling you that "the smart way to invest is to stick to investing in what you know". They don't invest in what they know, they find out what's going to make a lot of money, and then they learn about it. And if you want to be a successful investor, you'll have to do that too.

Even More Lies

I'm afraid we're going to have to talk some more about the "Wall Street Lies", mainly because there're so many of them. 'Invest in what you know' is just the tip of the iceberg. Here's another one that they call 'technical analysis'. It's the idea of watching and following the patterns, and watching the direction, and support levels, and resistance levels. If you were here with me, I could show you graphs and charts and pictures, but I know you're smart enough to use your imagination and follow along. It's probably better this way because if you can imagine it in your own mind, you'll understand it better.

Let's say there's a pattern of a particular stock, and you've seen it before… there's a chart with this wavy line, and it's going up, and the stock is gradually getting more expensive. And every couple of weeks or every month, the stock makes a new high as it's on this uptrend. Now they draw another line under the whole thing and in many cases the curve of that line will hit a bottom - they call that the support level. And then there's another line along the top, and they call that the resistance level.

Now, many of these technical analysts believe that the smart thing to do is to watch that pattern. And when it gets down to the bottom of that pattern, when it touches the line, you've now come to a good entry point. And you should buy it then. Then when it gets to the top of the line, that's an exit point and you should sell it.

But as you well know, humanity doesn't move in patterns. You might believe in the idea of patterns, but your husband or wife may be doing something that breaks the patterns, and the idea falls apart.

I had a lesson in my top tier professional training that I used to give to the very best analysts, the ones who really want to make it a career and get really good at it. I showed them that same picture using the S&P 500 with the wavy line moving up. So I added the line along the bottom of it. And you look at that line as I had it drawn, and they'd say, "What do you mean, this technical analysis doesn't work? Look at how that line shows you exactly where the turning points are".

They all felt pretty good about that... I'd even drawn in some arrows pointing to the spot at which this stock price came down and touched that line and then went up again. Again, they were baffled that I'd said it doesn't work. I asked them to give me a minute.

I made another picture of the same thing, drawing the same line. But then I put arrows in showing the times when it didn't bounce off that line. Either it didn't get down there, it turned back up before it got there, or it went through that line under it... it didn't stop and go up at that point. And they were just as many arrows where it didn't hit that line as there were where it did.

You see what you want to see. And you can set something up for someone to believe in just by drawing it a certain way. The fact is it works sometimes, and at other times it doesn't work. And if you take the times that you lose and subtract them from the times you win, you come out not doing very well at all.

But there are much better methods than guessing what the herd is going to do, the ones who are just following each other. I always keep in mind what I heard from my mentor, the specialist who was teaching me about the New York Stock Exchange. He's pointed out that things had been going up for 150 years, and still ninety percent of the people investing were losing their money. It's hard to even figure out a formula to lose money on something so obvious.

But instead of knowing what they're investing in, investing in a few things they've studied and understand, they're trying to guess what each other is going to do through pattern recognition. As I'd been taught at fourteen, if that kind of thing worked, if pattern recognition worked, these guys would know what their wives were going to do the next day at the mall.

People don't follow patterns. Really... I mean, we're not ants! Sometimes we do. Sometimes we don't. Sometimes we are purposely deceptive. But in the long run, if I want to know where that line is going, here are the facts; if a company is providing products or services that the world needs and they're doing it profitably, and growing their clientele, I can tell you that consistently, one hundred percent of the time, it is going to be reflected in the price of their stock.

Not necessarily today, or this week, or even this month - but when you look at it from year to year, if the company's worth more because it made more money for its owners, the stock price is higher. People are logically going to pay more for a company that's worth more. So if I figure out how much the company is going to be worth in the future by figuring out how much they're going to sell, I mean... it's really not rocket science, is it?

Instead of trying to figure out a pattern and outsmart other people, just use your brain. Let me give you a good working metaphor. You see that I often refer to the 'herd' mentality, and I want you to get a good picture of it. After all, we're talking about a herd, so imagine if you will a herd of cattle, or a bunch of cows, chasing around after one another in a pasture or an open field... here's how I'd use my brain.

Let's say feeding time. Now instead of me chasing around in the pastures or the meadows and trying to catch them to herd them back to the barn… what if I start giving them good grain, good food at the barn every day at around five o'clock? Well once they're trained and know that there's going to be good food for them at the barn, I don't have to chase them around anymore! I can just put the feed out and sit there at the barn at five o'clock, whistling or whittling or whatever, and just wait for them to show up.

That's really what's happening with these companies. Everyone's investing in them to make money. So instead of me chasing around guessing what they're going to do in the interim, when it's not clear what's going on, I can just wait patiently and give myself enough time. And if the company I'm interested in is worth more money because it's selling more and making more profit, then given time, the stock price is going to reflect that.

So I can just wait for the herd to come around. I base my buying or selling of the stock on how much the company's worth, based on the profits it earns, and how much those are growing, instead of just trying to guess based on their 'patterns' of behavior. So that's how you make money reliably. And the idea of pattern recognition is just another one of those "Wall Street Lies".

IN THE HEADLINES: GATES OPENS WINDOWS (FILM AT 11)

In the Headlines: Gates Opens Windows (Film at 11)

At one time, not long ago, the world relied on complicated, sequential, and difficult-to-learn language routines to give directions to their computers. Then Bill Gates and some friends devoted their lives to coming up with an innovative way for people to use simple graphics to give orders to their computers. All the computer geeks in my life at the time told me that this invention Gates had come up with (Windows) was a waste of time. You just didn't need it, they told me. Gates and friends didn't listen. They were rewarded. They became some of the richest people in the world.

Ten years from now, the richest man or woman in the world will run a nanotechnology or genetic engineering company that doesn't yet exist, selling a product that hasn't yet been invented. But I can assure you that the company, and the inventions it brings to humanity, will be helping many people get something they really, really want. And I assure you it will be financed by the same stock market that has been keeping me happy, busy, and rich for a lifetime.

How to Get Rich – Methods One & Two

Did you ever wonder how or why rich people in the United States get rich? That's a fair question, and the answer is amazingly simple. Those people get rich because they do something the world wants and needs. They either invent something, or they create a business as an entrepreneur, then build it up and run it properly. In many cases it's done with very little capital. In our society that's very possible and to a certain extent it's somewhat common. But there's another path to riches. It also takes work, but not the same kind of work.

Some people become very rich by owning a piece of a company that belongs to someone else... a company that produces things that people want and need, a company that's committed to supplying those needs. Most often, it's the kind of things that people need in order to have the lifestyle they want.

By investing in a company that dominates in its industry, one that can supply these products or services, a person like you can make a good profit on the company's success. I'm talking about a company that satisfies the customers who stay with them, customers who continue to buy again and again... then you have a company that is consistently increasing in value, because its sales and its profits are consistently growing in value.

Now, once you've identified that company, the next thing you have to do is to try to get as much leverage as possible. That means you want to invest in that company at the best possible price, and you want to do it with the biggest amount of your investment money that you can. You want to own the biggest possible piece of that company. So there's your simple answer.

Method two is the one I like. It's how rich people get really rich. They take advantage of the fact that we have no ceiling in our economy. There's nothing to stop you from going very, very far. We live in an auction market, where people buy the things they want the most, and the people who want them more than other people will offer more money. So the more they want it and the better you do your part, the more profits you can earn. You say you don't know how to do that? Stick with me, because at this stage in my life, I'm committed to doing everything in my power to show you how.

This has always been the formula for making yourself rich in a free economy. You identify something that people are committed to. Something they need in order to create the life they want. If you can produce what people want, and you can produce it at a good price, they'll want it and you'll make a good profit on it.

From there, you can increase production, and you can expand and attract more capital. You can become rich, and there's nothing to stand in your way. Well, almost nothing.

There's your own attitude and belief in yourself, plus your expectations of success. So the way to do it is to create a company that does something new and better than everybody else does it, and then stick with it, and build it up. That's one very good way to make yourself rich.

But another way to do it, and this is actually my preference, is to identify one by one companies that are producing goods or services that people want and need to create the life they want. The process of making your investments, of allowing your investments to make you rich, is to insightfully identify those goods and services that people are committed to having.

You should identify those goods and services to the point where the company you choose has beat the competition in its industry and is now one of the dominant producers. They are what we simply call the winners, distributing their product or service around the world to a growing global audience.

You can come into our wide-open capitalist system, take small amounts of money (or large amounts of money) and invest in that company by buying shares of their stock. You can grow with them and accumulate equity in their success. And it works even better for the smart investors who figure out ways to use leverage.

Let's Talk Leverage. The simplest example I can give is rental property. If I want to buy a ten-unit apartment complex, I can put down ten or twenty percent. Or if I'm well-established I can put down as little as five percent and borrow the other ninety-five percent from the bank.

If I'm making fifteen percent a year in profit on the rent and paying the mortgage off at four percent or even less, now I have a large equity holding in a big piece of real estate that generates a lot of income. It's very common - using leverage in the real estate business is something that everybody knows about and thinks about. It's considered to be one of the best and most reliable businesses you can be in. But the fact is you and I can do the same thing with any business.

The way we used to do it was to identify the company we wanted to own and buy shares of stock. In order to be able to buy three or four times as much stock, we could always borrow money at the bank. So picture a broker… he has something called a margin account which allows him to lend you enough to buy twice as much stock as you could afford on your own… now you can get twice as much of the company.

If you have equity in a property, you can borrow money from the bank, but actually if you have equity in anything, you can borrow money for it. And like real estate, you can borrow as much as ninety percent to buy the stock you want. And you end up with twice as much, maybe even three or four times as much. All to own a piece of a company that's producing profits by doing things people want and need.

You end up with a big piece of the company's stock using the ingenuity of borrowed money. That company may be growing at twenty or thirty percent a year, and in the past, you may have paid five or six percent interest on the borrowed money. But now, we don't even have to do that anymore because as of 1997 the exchanges started to offer stock options. It started in Chicago by the way… but this allowed you to make a deal for the rights to buy a stock later at a certain guaranteed price.

Is this good for us? Some say no – but they lie. This is in fact, great for you and me as investors. But why would the investment banking/brokerage business want to "dumb down" the investment strategies? Why would they train their people to tell you that you're too dumb to try to own specific companies because that isn't a winning strategy?

They tell you it makes no sense to own a specific company that's doing important things and growing with it... why? Why would a big company like Goldman Sachs or Morgan Stanley or Prudential securities train their people to tell you that you're too dumb to pick out a good company, get a good deal on it and stick with it as it grows?

If you think about it, that's exactly what they do with their money. So why would they ever tell you that it's not a good idea? That instead, you should own hundreds of baskets with one egg in each of them. In other words, why would they tell you that you should buy index funds and forget about trying to understand and own specific companies that are doing important things? Companies that you believe in, that are gaining great acceptance, and have sales growing at thirty, forty percent a year with exploding profits? Why, why, why??

There are a couple of good reasons for the business model they've developed. It's a great business model for them because they're the financial planners or advisors for millions of middle-class individuals. They also provide advisement services and management services for rich people... but the method by which they invest their own money is very, very different. They're there to make a lot of money, not to play defense and make a few bucks.

They have the whole world convinced that owning specific companies that do great things and growing with them is a bad idea, and it doesn't work. How in the world have they been able to do that? Ah-ha! They've convinced the media, and they've convinced the regulators and all the authors who write about investments, and all the business departments in all the universities, and the story gets repeated over and over again. And isn't it true that if you've heard a story a million billion times, day in and day out – isn't it easy to see how people come to believe it as fact?

The guys who start these untruths, these lies, they argue that the average investment manager doesn't know how to beat the market, and so you should just let him or her invest your hard-earned money in a diversified portfolio of index funds. They say the average Joe isn't going to beat that anyway.

Looks like we've opened up another can of lies, right? Well, here we go again... they say that great companies inventing important new technologies aren't going to make tons of money and naturally, their investors aren't going to get rich. But if you understand that there's a world-wide effort to get electricity to two or three billion people over the next few years, you'd know that it's going to take enormous amounts of copper wire to do that. So the smart people want to own copper mining and distributing companies, because they in fact, are going to see big growing profits. The products they sell are going to escalate in price and you can make a lot of money by owning some of that company's stock. And as I've said, if you could use a lot of leverage to own a bigger piece of that company, then naturally you're going to make even more money.

Why would a big investment bank that wants to put its huge amounts of money into companies that are successful - since they want to do that with their capital - why do they tell you it's not a good idea to do that with your capital? Of course it's easy for them to convince millions of people not to do that, because they've already convinced the business departments at the universities, and they've written so much about it, that this belief is now ubiquitous. Why would they pass that Wall Street lie on to the good people around them? Are they really just plain liars?

Forgive them; they know not what they do.

The answer is this; the people that are telling these lies, like your financial planner… they just don't know any better. They've been trained that way by the company they work for. But if you think about the economics of this, a big firm like a Goldman Sachs - or

A Morgan Stanley or Merrill Lynch or Edward D, Jones - I don't really want to single out a particular company, but clearly, if they want to have millions of investors under advisement, they can't lead those investors to buy the companies that they themselves want to own. Let me give you the obvious answer as to why.

There isn't enough stock in those prime companies for all of the millions of investors. They don't want to tell you about it because there just isn't enough equity to go around, even though their customers are paying them and assuming they're being given the best advice! If on the other hand they're selling the concept of the diversified portfolio, they can sell it to literally millions of people. It's just not practical for them to advise millions of middle-class people to buy the best companies. Period.

The techniques I'm offering here are based on the same techniques I discuss with my students - people who want to learn the specifics of exactly how to go about the leveraging methods I've talked about here. Now, just for the sake of an example, I want to talk to you about some of the tools we use. Of course, you're going to need a brokerage firm to make these investments for you. Do I care which brokerage firm you choose? Not in the least, but I don't mind telling you that in our classes, we use TD Ameritrade.

A couple of things I like about them; first, there's a great piece of free software they offer called ThinkOrSwim. It's easy, and with everyone in my classes using the same software, we're all on the same page. I use it with them to demonstrate a lot of specifics. And second, you don't actually have to invest any real money with TD Ameritrade as you're learning (unless you want to), but rather it allows you to open a 'practice' account.

For those students, and probably for you too, the job is to practice until you get really good at this. By the way, it's always been my policy that even after the instruction, if they still don't quite get it, I stick with them, offering additional help until they say "OK, I've got it now." That's when I know they're confident and I've done a good job. But again, you should not be investing real money until you've practiced and know what you're doing.

I don't actually do the transactions for them... I'm just here to show that it's not rocket science and if you've got half a brain, I can show you how to use it. Now, I've been using the same techniques for many years. But the reason I've made it my latest mission to teach this method is because as of this writing (in 2021), we're facing the greatest opportunity of my long lifetime. It's also the greatest opportunity of your lifetime! Because a lot of things are happening right now, all at the same time.

As we've stated numerous times, the world shut down because of COVID. And the news people love to report on are all the obstacles - the recent talk is about new variants of COVID. They say this side effect or that one is happening, and this country isn't getting enough vaccine, etc. But what's actually happening, as you and everyone knows, is that the world is rebuilding.

Gradually, more and more people are taking the vaccines, or they've had the virus and some never show any symptoms. Many of them didn't even know they had it. But as immunity spreads, the world is going back to doing the things that people love to do. Here in the United States, we're a little ahead of most places... the U.S., Israel, and England are about sixty percent there. Other countries are gradually catching up too - Europe, at around thirty or forty percent. Then there's

Asia, behind Africa, and behind them, South America… but everybody's working they're way out of this. And as they do, they're going back to doing the things that they've always loved to do.

That means they spend more money, they buy things, they go places in a very predictable way because whatever they used to do is what they're going back to. However, while this is going on, the destruction of paper money presents an enormous opportunity. Now when I say the destruction of paper money, every industrialized country, in fact just about everyone around the world is trying to jumpstart their economies.

They need to help their populations make it through the closings caused by COVID, and address the stopping of virtually all activity. In order to help everybody get through that, they've been literally printing money, albeit fictitious money. For so many years, paper money hasn't been attached to any real asset. It used to be that paper money simply represented each country's holdings of gold and silver.

Remember that during the time of Richard Nixon, there was a global agreement to discontinue the connection of paper money to gold, so that each currency floated on its own, and was worth whatever it was worth next to the other currencies. So that was done in a fairly responsible way by most countries.

But as you probably know, since the advent of the pandemic, in order to jumpstart their economies, every country including the United States has been creating more and more money. As of mid 2021, the United States alone had created more than three trillion dollars. We talk about trillions now… in a very casual way. And we've become accustomed to it!

If you think back over the last couple of years, you never really heard of anybody creating trillions of anything. And one thing is for certain, when you create trillions of dollars, the dollar is not very scarce, is it? The whole idea of currency should be that there's a limited amount of it. And in the U.S. that new paper money has absolutely nothing behind it. In Europe, they're up to about three trillion as well. That's more than six trillion dollars of paper money in the Western world alone. And now they're contemplating all kinds of new ways to create even more paper money!

Again, when you create trillions of anything, it isn't really all that scarce. It's a fact that the value of paper money is declining. That means that the value of everything else, particularly things that you can't just create on paper, things that you have to actually make… everything with a limited supply is worth more, in your paper money. We calculate values in dollars, in Japan they calculate in yen, in Europe its Euros, in England it's pounds. But wherever you are, the value of the paper money is diminished, and therefore everything else costs more. What you should get from all of that is a very predictable increase in the value of everything that's scarce.

You know, these things that we say people want and need – well, it's mostly new stuff. Digital stuff, high-tech stuff. In the recent past, the U.S. has been mostly responsible for these inventions, innovations, and ideas. But now they're coming from everywhere, including China and Europe. Worldwide, they're coming up with new and better ways of doing things. Sometimes we do it using artificial intelligence and all kinds of new computerized ways of counting and calculating things. And while only a few of us are creating these things, the whole world wants to use these techniques.

If you're a company and you want to efficiently communicate with your customers there's no better way to do it than to have a computer answering the telephone. You might say you hate it, but you'd hate it even more if you had to wait forever for someone to just answer the phone! Now, the computer answers the phone and routes the calls to the right department where you actually get to talk to the right person. That's just a simple example of something being done digitally that was always done manually. And the part of our world that doesn't have it yet wants it, and they want it now!

If you want to see it for yourself, let me explain what's going on in some parts of this planet. This is a big part of the process that I use in my classes, because before you invest, you really need to do some due diligence and study some of the trends that move things and move people. And you have to be patient. Hearing some of these teachings once doesn't mean it all sinks in immediately. In fact, I record my online classes and then send a copy to every student. I encourage them to watch the class over and over if necessary to make sure they get it all. They get to stop, start, and pause the recording and create their own pace.

Remember the 5-step process? The first thing I teach is to identify the companies you'd like to invest in. How? Just imagine what's going on beyond your neighborhood. Think of the global opportunities staring at you. And don't be overwhelmed by thinking that you need to identify forty or fifty companies. Think more like five, or maybe ten that you really understand.

Then I teach how to evaluate them, how and where to do the research, to find all the things you need to know about these companies that you can actually own stock in. What follows is the mechanics of how to acquire your investments, a method to monitor each one, and finally, when and how to take profits

The market, as you know, is made up of companies that issue stock, and most people think that the idea of the stock market is to guess what everybody else is going to do. They're looking at charts and all kinds of ways to try to predict what everybody else is going to do, and they don't really understand very well what they're investing in.

And there are trends, so people follow the trends. They're like lemmings, following the herd with no real direction of their own. I personally am convinced that the better way is what I just identified above… the five steps that can help you get on the right path. Identify, evaluate, acquire, monitor, and take profits.

Here's What I See

What do you see when you look at the U.S. and more importantly, the rest of the planet? Here's what I see. About one quarter of the world now has electricity and lives pretty much the way we do. But now, more than three billion people in the world (soon to be four billion), have cell phones. They're using those smart phones to connect. Because of this amazing digital transformation, most of those people have the ability to watch videos, they get Netflix, they're connected to Amazon – they see how we live.

I recently saw a photo of a lady in India, living basically in a grass hut with a dirt floor, with chickens walking in and out, and yet because of her cell phone, she knows how we live. She and all of her neighbors all over India are determined to have the lifestyle we have. I was in India about ten years ago, and you could ride from one big city to the next, and in between, it was dark. There was no electricity between the big cities for those people who lived in the small villages.

Now, over the last few years in the electrification process in India and in fact, all around the world, they've spread a grid. And of course, that grid of wiring uses lots and lots of copper. So they generate electricity and that grid goes to each little village now. They're very proud of the fact that every little village in India has got electricity. There's a telephone pole with a step down transformer, but almost none of the people have electricity to their homes yet!

Let's look to the future. By the end of the next 10 years, everyone in India is going to have electricity in their homes. And again, this is happening all over the world. There are many predictable changes that are taking place. Among them is the fact that it takes massive amounts of copper to wire all these houses. That's easily predictable. That need for copper is tied directly to the desires of those who want desperately to have what we Americans have. That's because they may not have internet service in the house as of yet, but more and more, they own cell phones.

You can see now what I mean by a digital transformation. You can see that although the cultures are diverse all around the world, they're becoming more and more like us because now they can see how we live, and they want to live that way too. This digital transformation is an amazing opportunity. And the companies! They know the best way to reach their customers is digitally. And so every company is developing methods of doing that. And companies all around the world are imitating how we communicate in our country with our customers.

Count the opportunities: ONE, you have the rebuilding after COVID. TWO, you have the destruction of paper money, where everything you can't print is worth more. And THREE, the entire world is engaged in a digital transformation. That woman in the photo in India is going to need a bank. She may move to a more advanced village. I can't say exactly which country is going to run her bank, but I do know she's going to have an ATM, they're going to have debit cards and credit cards, and they're going to be connected to Visa and MasterCard and Square. I know that every family there wants to have computers, they want their kids to go to college, they want them to become doctors and lawyers and accountants... and this is happening steadily around the world.

This lightning-fast process hit a bump in the road, it's true. But now COVID has a cure rate around the world. Even India is up to about fifteen to twenty percent of their people being immunized, and they're in a gigantic campaign to get everybody immunized. As they do, they're going back to the lightning-fast progress they were making before the pandemic. And as I've said, this is all enormously predictable.

Everyone, please step up onto the platform

I want to take a minute out here to explain what a platform company is, because it's going to help you quite a bit in understanding the economics. If you were Coca-Cola, and you want to produce more Coca Cola, you want to expand and grow… and by the way, this isn't just about making soda – it applies to making rubber balls or ink pens or virtually anything else. The economics are the same no matter what.

It takes a lot of infrastructure; it takes a factory and machines and people to deliver it. It takes trucks and all kinds of stuff. So if you are in the normal economy like we've had over the last 1000 years, and you wanted to make more Coca Cola, you're going to need more syrup, and more bottles, and more machines and more people and more trucks. It would take a lot of investment, a lot of borrowed money to be able to expand the business.

But now we've started to invent digital products. Take Microsoft. When they created that computer giant, they had to learn how to program the computers. This is the way it was in the late 70s and the early 80s. And all computers worked through a system called DOS. It was a list of instructions that you had to give to the computer in perfect order. And if it wasn't perfect, it wouldn't work.

I got out of the Marine Corps in 1965 and went straight to college. Computers were a whole new thing. But the computers were massive, like the size of a room. We had to learn how to program them by punching little holes in little cards and it had to be in perfect order.

By 1980, you could have your own personal computer, but you still had to program it and give it instructions in perfect order. And if it was out of sequence in any way, if you made any kind of a mistake, any kind of a little spelling error, if everything wasn't perfect, it wouldn't work. And so it was very hard for people to use.

So here comes a bunch of kids – I already mentioned Bill Gates and his friends – they went into a garage somewhere and came out with a way to program those instructions by using little pictures they called icons. And they created this idea of a mouse and with that mouse, you'd point to a picture that represented what you wanted the computer to do. All the steps of the programming were already in that computer and when you pointed to that icon, which anybody could do, that computer understood all the instructions. It would open the right program and carry out any task you wanted.

This was Microsoft's real contribution. And oh, what it did! It made the computer usable for anybody. But the important thing about that was this. Now, think about Microsoft - let's say they make ten copies of Windows, and Word, and Excel, which all of us use. And we have to subscribe, and we pay them a yearly subscription fee. But understand this; Microsoft is a platform.

They can make a billion copies of their software as easily as making a thousand copies. They don't need more trucks or buildings or anything, it's all digital. And so their cost of expansion is all spent on new research and development and marketing. Basically, they can produce as much of their software as they want, without really spending any new money.

So the economics of the platform company are more favorable and easier to expand, and easier to do than anything we ever had before that. MasterCard is another good example. MasterCard doesn't really lend money. It's just an electronic system and they can join into the banking system of new countries and now everybody can attach to the MasterCard system. But it doesn't take the kind of expansion that it takes to make more Coca Cola, because it's all software and they can produce more and more of it with no new money.

Fastly is another platform. If you're not familiar, I can explain what they do. Five or ten years ago, if you wanted to watch a movie on your television and you had Netflix, it would take it a half hour to load. And even during the movie, it would chatter and drop out and buffer. The source of that movie was far away and it had to be transported to your computer, your TV, or your receiver.

Fastly is a company that has an electronic means of moving information that's in the cloud to servers all over the world. The data from those servers gets to you because there are so many of them, and likely there's one or more very near to you. The data gets to you faster, and voila! No more buffering.

So that lady in the grass hut, and her neighbors? They can receive Amazon on their cell phone, and they can order stuff, just as well as they can watch a movie on Netflix. It reaches them as quickly as it reaches you or me. We're all so spoiled that we don't want to wait ten or twenty minutes. We want it now, and we don't want any buffering.

So Fastly is a platform that has servers all over the world, and if Amazon needs to build a complex application program, they put that program into the Fastly system. Fastly now has expanded to hundreds of subscribers like Amazon, and the expansion costs Fastly very, very little. That's what a platform company is.

There are lots of others too, like Twilio. If you use Uber or Lyft, you go to your phone. You find the number for a driver, you can see where his car is on a map, you email or text him, etc. All of these different methods of communication take different kinds of code. And Twilio is the one platform that ties it all together, and lets companies communicate with their customers in all these different ways. So again, Twilio is a platform, and they can expand without any real infrastructure investment.

PRACTICE AND REPETITION

Practice and Repetition

Y ou may have heard some of the things we're discussing, but some of it is going to be new material, and it needs to sink in. You know, the way the brain works is it can develop neural pathways. I guess a good metaphor is to compare information coming to you like water overflowing its banks.

At first, it just doesn't really flow or go anywhere; it just seeps right into the ground. At first, the dirt impedes the flow, but as that area overflows, it soaks in and begins to dig a channel, it gets to move easier and easier, and slowly and gradually the little channel turns into a torrent and can actually become a river.

That's how the brain works when you learn something new. First it sort of impedes the flow, then it just sort of soaks in. As the brain gets more and more familiar with the information, it develops a neural pathway. It flows and gets easier as you use that neural pathway.

A lot of what I teach using this options method is new and you'd be surprised to know that almost nobody knows or understands it. Once you practice on a practice account, that's when you get to invest real money. At that point you'll come to realize that there are literally hundreds of millions of shares of a lot of companies available, but you'll see every day that there were only two or three transactions of the type that you're doing. And sometimes it's zero! People just don't know how to do this. And that's why it's so profitable. If everybody was bidding them up, they'd be more expensive, and it wouldn't be so easy to make money.

Learn this and you'll be one of very few people in the world that knows how to do it. This is about thinking. Of course, there are a bunch of other concepts that I teach so that my students understand the market that we're in at any given time. But the options method stands tall and virtually always pays off.

Now, you'll need to eliminate some of your conventional thinking. Your friends might tell you that you have to be 'diversified.' Or, they'll suggest that you need a financial planner to help you own a whole bunch of different stuff, because you're not smart enough to have a strategy of your own. But as you know by now, the big brokerage firms also have billions of dollars of their own money. And they have specialists up at the top of the Empire State Building or something and those people are actually doing specific transactions. They're not diversifying. They're doing transactions that make money because they know what they're doing.

If you have a bunch of different stuff, it's like having a thousand baskets with one egg in each basket. And that 'financial planner', who doesn't really know anything, can feel like an expert to you. His job is not to actually know something; his job is to teach you to diversify, which means you have no strategy at all. And this has been going on forever. That's not what we're doing here. This is actually about you knowing what you're investing in. This is how people become wealthy. This is how you change your life.

Weeding out the Weeds

Let's talk about a few of the companies that you might want to own. The ones that allow you to use a lot of leverage to own them the way that I described to you earlier. Remember that it's about how people take a small amount of money, have a strategy, lock in the right to own something, and then are able to benefit from it as it becomes worth a lot more money. So, what companies do you want to invest in?

Well, there are so many companies out there that are listed on the stock exchange, but the few that we want are a small percentage of what's available. Instead of searching for the ones we want, let's weed out the ones we don't want.

Remember, we only need five or ten companies to make us a lot of money. So, the first thing to check is to see if a company is or is not in one of the sectors based on the new digital transformation. I mean, a lot of the ones that are not in these sectors are in fact, good companies. From plumbing companies to movie theatres, there are lots of good ones. But we're not interested in those. We're looking for specific companies, we're looking for a sure thing where we can use a lot of leverage and ultimately make a difference in our own lives.

We want the companies that are benefiting from the decline in the value of paper money. The governments of all of the developed nations – America, Europe, and even China -they're creating enormous amounts of money. They print it and they distribute it. They're doing that to try to stimulate their economy, and that's okay. But as I've said, when you print trillions of anything, it's no longer scarce.

Normally, money has value because of the limited supply. But when there's an infinite amount of it around, it's worth less and less. Printing more just creates inflation, which means that each of those dollars or yen or whatever is worth less money. Everything you buy with it now costs more.

We want to benefit from companies that have pricing power, the ability to raise their prices and sell more... the companies that have a growing clientele around the world, the companies that are profitable because they do something unique. They have the ability to raise their prices so that they can keep up with inflation. We want a company like that. A company that's involved in the information explosion, the digital explosion, much like the platforms I've told you about. When they want to expand, they don't have to spend money on things like syrup and trucks and delivery people. They don't have that big cost of expansion.

Because of the digital transformation, we have such an easy spread of information. With that comes uniformity. Everybody in the world, learning from each other, is picking out all the best stuff. So, although there are lots of good companies in the world, we're going to pick only the companies that have the pricing power, the ones that benefit from the decline in the value of paper money, and are involved in the explosion of information around the world. Those are the fabulous platform businesses that don't have expenses except for the cost of research, development and marketing.

The next thing is we want a company that is a member of the oligarchy in their industry. That means they're one of the leading and most powerful companies in the industry that they're in. They're powerful and they're not going to be bullied by a bigger company.
These are the companies that control their own destiny.

Next, we want to make sure that they have easy access to very inexpensive capital. They can issue bonds and pay very low interest on those bonds. The banks are begging them to borrow money because they know they're a good risk, and the banks can see that they're a growing, powerful company. We invest in these companies because we want expansion.

We want them to grow, and we want to grow with them. If they have to keep issuing stock and bringing in more owners, they're diluting us. The prime candidate company for us can get all the capital they want by borrowing it cheap, or by issuing bonds. They can grow at twenty, thirty, or forty percent a year and pay three percent interest, rather than selling stock and taking on more partners that we have to share profits with.

Next, the company we want has to have superior skills and management. They have experienced people running the company that have been through good and bad times.

These people are very good at what they do. They create rising sales and rising profits. The number of people that are good customers for them is growing, and we can see their sales growing by leaps and bounds

Now sometimes, a company that we invest in may be investing a lot of money in marketing or research and development to get better and better at what they do. That's an investment, but they get to count it as an expense, and they get to write it off. So, it reduces their taxes.

Then too, a company may look like sales are up, but you might look on the internet and find that the company isn't profitable at all. What we want is to make sure that it is, even in relatively new companies that fit that mold. For each transaction that they do, the gross profit is very healthy; they make money on every transaction. So, we want rising sales, and we want profits.

One of the most important factors we look for in a company is that their intellectual property is extremely difficult to duplicate. We want them to be unique and have patents and copyrights and trademarks that prevent other companies from competing with them. Moderna is a good example. They're growing very rapidly because their medicine is patented. Other companies can't make that formula and compete with Moderna because there are patents.

One of the easiest ways to find this kind of company is to look for those intellectual property protections. They're doing things that other companies can't copy... another great example is Microsoft. There are also companies that are doing things that are not patented, but they're protected otherwise. Maybe they're the only ones that know how to do what they do, or they have special proprietary contacts. Here's an example.

American Tower makes those special towers for 5g. As the world gets 5g, the internet is faster, but it requires a special kind of tower, different from the ones they use now. There's going to be hundreds of thousands of those 5g towers, because they have to be very close to where you are in order for 5g to work. The thing is, American Tower is the company that built thousands of 4g towers all over the world. Their special contacts are their existing clients, such as AT&T and Verizon, as well as some of the best companies in Europe and Asia.

So even if you wanted to go into the tower business, you could build a tower, but they have all the customers, they've got special contacts. You and I couldn't succeed in the tower-building business because we don't have those existing contacts. We want to be very selective about choosing these companies and eliminate almost every other company in the world. We want a sure thing, or as close to a sure thing as we can get.

The 'S' Curve

Along the way I've asked you to imagine a graph so I could illustrate some points. I know, it's not easy. But bear with me once more. Even if you can't 'picture' the graph, the concept makes perfect sense anyway, and here it is.

This is about the S curve. At the bottom, moving left to right on a relatively straight horizontal line is where the company is in the innovation stage. They're successfully coming up with new ideas and products. But it's not necessarily a profitable stage.

Then the line begins to rise, turning back to the left, and as it does, the idea or products go into an acceptance stage. This is where people have noticed them and are in agreement with the ideas, and those ideas go to market. Finally at the top, the line curves around toward the right, begins to flatten out again, and this is where the idea or product moves into a saturation phase. Just remember, the innovation stage is where there's not a lot of money to be made. But a lot of people don't understand that the stock market is not about innovation and clever new ideas.

Whenever I do my radio program or a podcast, I get calls from people who ask what I think about this new kind of glass that some company invented. Maybe someone told them it's going to be used to make the new breed of cell phones. Or what do I think about this new kind of LED light, or this emerging new kind of medicine? They ask because they're thinking that to make money, they have to constantly be on the lookout for new ideas.

Remember, that's the bottom of the S curve, the innovation stage, where the new ideas are just being created. They haven't reached acceptance yet, and certainly are not anywhere near saturation. So at this early stage, there's no money and no profits to share. Note also that the cost of innovation is very high, and there is a race between companies trying to innovate, so it's very competitive. That stage of the product's lifecycle is very tough.

After they get to the point where most of the innovation is behind them, now they're on the rising line of acceptance. With new markets, and in our case a new world, companies like Microsoft and MasterCard have passed basic innovation and they're growing during this digital transformation. Everybody wants what they've got, and they're spreading around the world and more importantly, they're now very profitable. This area between innovation and saturation, this acceptance phase is where we make the money. And by the way, most of those other companies that were being innovative have lost. Microsoft and MasterCard have won.

If you're wondering why I have no interest in companies that are in the saturation stage, let me explain. I'm not really interested in owning or investing in Kroger or Albertsons or some other supermarket company, or Kraft

Mayonnaise. Those are good companies, and they're profitable. But don't expect a big move up over the next year or two. I'm looking for that phase where they're spreading around the world. Eventually, this kind of company hits the saturation phase, which again, is not particularly profitable. And that's why I'm not really that interested in them anymore.

How about that oil, Slick?

People have asked me how I knew back in 2020 that I should be investing in oil companies. Well, at that time, the price of oil was like nine or ten dollars a barrel. And it wasn't very profitable - the oil business had not been profitable for a long time. In fact a lot of companies were failing. Plus, the banks didn't want to lend them money. Investors didn't want to invest in the oil business… a lot of people had lost a lot of money in that industry. A lot of oil companies, drillers, and pipeline companies were going bankrupt because it had come to a point where it was just too crowded. Ah-ha… saturation.

When we see something that the world wants and needs, but it's in this phase where it's too crowded, that's when the prices are very cheap. And new companies aren't jumping in. It's hard for them to get capital and they're out of favor. And that's where oil companies were back in 2020 at nine or ten dollars a barrel. So, it wasn't particularly profitable, and nobody wanted to invest in it at that time.

But we know that the lifespan goes like this; those companies that made it and were still in business, they bought up better leases, better land, and they got the best employees. They got to buy up everybody else's equipment for pennies on the dollar because companies were going out of business.

You can see that it's now becoming better and better - because there's not that many companies competing, the price of oil starts to go up, which we've seen happen. As the price of oil goes up, the oil becomes more and more profitable.

Oil is starting to look pretty good. It's getting so profitable that it's starting to become a 'hot sector'. They talk about it on TV and investors are jumping in. It's attracting big money.

Brokers are calling their clients and telling them that there's a lot of money flowing in here, the price of oil is going up, so the prices of products that are made from oil also go up. It's attracting a lot of capital, and it's a great invest-ment. Well, remember, we got in there when the price was nine or ten dollars. As of mid-2021 it's gone up to twenty-five or thirty dollars! My, my… all of that is such good news. But… you should recognize that this is really the beginning of the end.

Oh, for now we're still there and still making a fortune. The price of oil is up there and still moving up. And there's more and more demand, even with prices flirting with thirty or even thirty-five dollars. HA! In the short time it's taken to write these few pages, oil prices are soaring again. I just heard it's up to over eighty dollars a barrel, and everyone predicting that a hundred dollars a barrel is in plain sight. By the time you read this, who knows? But the companies that we own - the ones that lived through it at the low price point and bought up all the equipment and the leases? They're getting more and more profitable and attracting more and more capital.

But eventually… and you probably saw this if you were watching back in 2000. This same thing happened with the technology industry. It happened in Silicon Valley with all those new inventions. They were attracting capital. They were getting more and more valuable. There were internet companies and software companies, and it was all growing, attracting more and more investors. Everybody was buying companies like Microsoft, Sun Microsystems, Intel, and a lot of us were making a fortune back in nineteen ninety-nine.

But eventually… everybody starts to hear about it - investment banking companies and brokers are attracting more and more money. And suddenly we have so much money flowing into that industry, there's so much capacity that the capacity is outgrowing the demand for the product. It was growing because of all the demand and it was so profitable. But as more and more people are investing in it... well, there's the inevitable eventuality.

You saw this happen, not only with the technology crash of two thousand. You also saw it happen in twenty fifteen - the oil business got too crowded. It attracted so many investors that the industry and the capacity were growing faster than the demand. So now the new companies that borrowed a lot of money to get into that business were having trouble because now there's no pricing power.

There's so much competition in that industry that the companies that are new start to cut the price. And once they start to cut the price, everybody has to cut their price and the prices start moving down and becoming less and less profitable. And eventually some companies begin to sell assets to try to stay in business. And now the value of the assets is going down faster than they can liquidate their debt. They're hitting this debt cycle, and this is what we call a crash, or the liquidation phase.

This is where oil was around twenty-fifteen through twenty-seventeen. And this is what happened to the technology companies that crashed back in year two thousand. Of course, Microsoft had continued to grow and has become one of the most profitable companies in the history of the world.

I live in Texas, and I know a little bit about the oil companies, I grew up with people in the oil business; my kids went to school with people in the oil business. We know that when the price of oil was very low, the whole world was beginning to expand, and in order to expand, the whole world has to have electricity.

They're going to have to burn oil to generate electricity. And we knew that the demand was going to rise faster than the supply. At that point where all those companies were going out of business, crashing and liquidating, we returned to a time when prices are cheap, the industry is out of favor. And the few companies that survive are making big profits. They're selling something that everybody needs. And so the cycle continues. And we can benefit from it over and over again. We're able to take advantage of that and recognize the different stages at which this is happening.

Chapter

09

A MAN WALKS DOWN THE STREET... AND TURNS INTO A STOCK EXCHANGE

A Man Walks Down the Street... and turns into a Stock Exchange

I grew up in Lower Manhattan, very near the New York Stock Exchange which was about a mile or so away. When I was very young my grandfather would hold my hand as we walked the short distance to the Stock Exchange. And all the kids in our project, we weren't rich. All we could think about was, how are we going to get out of this project?' How are we going to make a life for ourselves? And most of the kids were planning to either go play baseball for the Yankees or become professional boxers or something, anything to make a lot of money and get out of the project. We were young and we didn't really know the importance of education.

But my grandfather was a very smart guy who had come to the U.S. because he'd heard about this free economy. And he said to me, "You're probably not going to make it to the Yankees, and you probably won't be a professional boxer". But as we stood there on the floor of the Stock Exchange he said, "This can be your way out of these projects. This is the way you can actually become wealthy".

He was also an author with a great gift of gab, and he was able to talk his way into getting his grandson into the back door to hang around on the floor of the New York Stock Exchange. So they used to let me come there. I could skip school and go down and hang around there. The other guys on the floor kind of adopted me, and I was sort of like a mascot. By the time I was fourteen or fifteen years old, I realized I was the only kid that was allowed down there. Mostly I'd go for coffee for the guys. But they used to teach me a lot about what was going on.

There was this one guy who was sort of my mentor - he was actually the specialist for Polaroid at that time. And he said to me, "Look at this. This thing's been going up for a hundred and fifty years. So how is it possible that ninety-five percent of these people end up losing money?" He posed the question, and he also gave me the answer. " It's because those ninety-five percent thought of the stock market the same way they thought of a casino… they were basically lazy, they didn't really know anything about the companies they'd invest in. They were just betting on when the market would go up and when it would go down. They were gamblers".

In reality, they were trying to guess what each other was doing. They treated it like a game. And this guy explained to me that this is not a stock market, this is not a casino. This is not about guessing what everybody else is going to do. It's about understanding a company. And it's about understanding that companies come here to raise money, to get partners, to raise capital, so that they can expand. I know. Some of those companies are just junk. But some of them do the things that the world will absolutely want and need. And your job is to just know about a few of those.

Like I said, this guy was a specialist in Polaroid and he knew everything about it. He would always make money, because he knew when to buy it and when to sell it and what it was worth. And everybody buying Polaroid had to buy that stock from him. He's right there in the middle of it. And he's getting huge leverage because millions of dollars of Polaroid stock are going through him. And that's how he made money. And what I learned was that the stock market is not about guessing what other people are going to do. It's about investing in companies.

There were times like back in… I guess it was the 'year-2k'. I was managing assets at that time, and it was still fairly early in my career. I had about eighty million dollars under management, and I was just starting to make a good living. And at that time, the interest rate started to go up. Well, the central bank, the Fed, had printed a lot of money and was beginning to worry about inflation. And the tech stocks were going higher and higher. And the Fed started to raise interest rates to slow the economy and protect it from inflation. I don't mind telling you that I lost about $30 million. And I realized that if I was going to be in this business investing for other people, they were going to fire me if they were losing a lot of money. And we had just lost $30 million.

But I realized that there's one more piece to this puzzle. I'd have to be able to identify the difference between a little pullback, and a real serious bear market. That all comes down to the supply and demand for stocks. We call it buying power and selling pressure. You don't have to know how to calculate all this. There are a lot of components that go into it. I keep track of it on something I call the Market X-Ray… other people use it too. They subscribe to it because they depend on it to determine when there's going to be a bear market, they want to know for sure when we're in a bull market, they need that confidence to be able to tolerate some corrections.

I'll go into this elsewhere in this book, but the only reason I bring it up now is there's a need to understand that bear markets can potentially last for ten or fifteen years. Think about the people that were investing in 1929. The market was at 380 and then they lost as much as eighty percent of their value. And your 'financial planner' would say, "Oh, I know, it's going down, but don't worry… it always comes back up".

Right. It always comes back. But sometimes it takes five years or ten years. You know, the people back in 1929 didn't get back up to 380 until around 1950. Before those people got back to even, they were unfortunately dead. So you don't have to worry about every little fluctuation. And the markets are going to fluctuate, because they're made up of those crazy people who think they're in a casino, trying to guess what others are doing.

And here you are, investing in companies that you can begin to understand. You know that when there's an overriding bear market, where the whole stock market goes down and pulls everything down, and the economy goes into a recession, you don't really want to be sticking around. You don't know if it's going to be two years or five years, or ten years. So bear markets are to be avoided. And you need to be able to tell the difference between fluctuations and a bear market.

Here's another little history lesson. You may remember the crash in the stock market in 2008. Well, in 2007, I used to be a regular every week on the Closing Bell on CNBC, and on the Neil Cavuto show on Fox. And I remember it was October of 2007, and the Dow Jones Industrial Average hit 14,000 that day. They were having this huge celebration, flooding your TV screen with confetti, and everybody was so excited that the Dow had hit 14,000.

But right after that, selling pressure started to rise. Right there at the beginning the stock market was still going up, all the way through the beginning of 2008. But I started to see danger because I could see the selling pressure starting to rise. I've been studying this for years. And I could see that it wasn't fluctuating, that selling pressure was having a sustained, significant move up. After just a matter of months of this rise in selling pressure, you begin to get very, very vulnerable. And any little thing can set it off and start a bear market that can last for years.

Now as I said, in December of 2007 I was right there on the floor of the New York Stock Exchange, right after that selling pressure started to rise. If you go look at the stock market at that time, you'll see that the bull market continued into 2008, and stocks continued to be strong. Buying power was rising, but selling pressure was still rising too. This went on for months and I started to see the danger. I'd started to lighten up a little bit on stocks. Now we get to the summer of 2008. Selling pressure has been going up for a long time.

We're coming up to July of 2008. One of my customers was a friend of mine, and he came over and said look, I'd like to remain friends. But I'm going to move my money to somebody else. My small cap fund has gone up 16% and I see you starting to get conservative. Well, that was in July of 08. You may remember that the stock market was still okay. But…

In September we had the big crash. Really big. We called it a global financial crisis. The Fed had raised interest rates and the value of houses got stuck. The banks had bought a whole bunch of mortgage bonds on credit. Then, two things happened. Suddenly, not only did selling pressure go up, but buying power started to go down. And this crash lasted for years. This is why I watch my Market X-ray.

As of this writing in 2021 the Market X-ray tells me that things are very, very volatile. But although it may be going up and it may be going down, at least it's got a direction that you can read. There's a trend. The COVID year was very different, but everyone understands why. It's been difficult, but heading into 2022, we're heading toward the end of that. Still, the market is very moody, and demand for stocks has been falling for some time… so I think we may see a bit more of a pullback. And if the stock market could get down maybe ten or fifteen percent, it could be a very good opportunity for us to duplicate a lot of the big gains that we had in 2020.

LOOKING AHEAD

Looking ahead

Now, you don't have to be an expert at this. But the bottom line is, we can see that we're about to have another very exciting opportunity where there's a pause, and then there's a selling episode. We may have another really good entry point where we can make a lot of money again. Hopefully, as you're reading this, you're getting the idea and learning how to take advantage of it. But I wanted you to see that this is not random. This is not a casino.

We're not in the business of just guessing what everybody else is going to do… we're picking out specific companies. We want to take advantage of this little correction, and by the time you've done this with a practice account, and you've become adept at using the principles… heck, you may be able to catch a really good opportunity to duplicate the gains that we had back in October and November of 2020… and the very strong gains that we had back in March of 2020. Hope this didn't get a little tedious, but I just wanted you to see and understand what's going on there beneath the surface.

It's true. They lie… but why, why?

I've said before that the big money manager are guilty of trying to make you feel like you're too stupid to have a strategy the way they do. They want to see you with an egg in each of a bunch of baskets. But we didn't talk about why they do that. I mean let's face it, there's a conspiracy to have you believe that.

Another good question, why does that idea get spread throughout the media? Even the schools teach that the only way to invest is to be very diversified. That way you can be pretty wrong all the time, but not always totally wrong. Well one thing is true… that's absolutely a lie. But if it's so wrong, why do they do it?

I already explained that this isn't how they handle their money. Google some images of the big brokerage firms and you'll see pictures of a bunch of MBAs sitting in a room surrounded with multiple computers and screens. They're actually doing a lot of real original research. They're very careful about which specific stocks they invest in. And I've got to tell you that if you look at their financial performance, you'll see that they make most of their money on two things. They make money by charging you commissions on their dealings with you, and they make money by trading for their own accounts, investing their own money.

Again, they're very careful. They know everything about every company that they invest in. They don't buy index funds. They don't just throw their money into diversified bonds and things like that. They buy the things they believe in and they evaluate and know everything about them.

So after you realize that the growing companies are the ones supplying the world with what it wants and needs, how do you find out who's doing that? Well, this is America, where we have a free market. And out of necessity it's also a much-regulated market. When it comes to money, if listed companies lie about their accounting, they go to jail. You've seen it happen. This is one of the places in our system where you can actually trust your research and know the information that you get is truthful and correct.

If you were anywhere else in the world, whether it's China or Guatemala, and you were trying to figure out what company to invest in, you'd probably have to go and have lunch with the guy who owns that company - more than once or twice. You'd need to get to know him and decide if you can trust him, because outside of the U.S., there's a lot of fiction out there. You have to really know the people you're investing with. The beauty of our system is that it's so well regulated. We've set up systems that guarantee that people have to tell the truth. They're regulated, they get audited, and if they don't tell the truth, they end up in jail.

Trust your research and know that you can actually invest in a specific company and be confident that you know the real story about them. That's how all the big brokerage houses do it… they use those very smart specialists to do all that research for them. Then, when they take those companies public, they do exactly the kind of thing that we're learning how to do here. They take an option, they have the right to own a big piece of that company, and they bought it at the starting price. They had the knowledge and they had the connections. (But they're still telling you that you have to be diversified).

You not only have to find companies supplying the world with what it needs, you have to find the ones that are the very best at it. Who's got the best technology, the best ideas, and the best operation? Then audit them and make sure that they're doing it profitably. How much profit do they make on each transaction? What's their gross profit, or their gross margin?

Oh, and to answer the question of why they do that - they're protecting their own interests. Remember that they have hundreds of thousands and sometimes millions of clients in those big brokerage firms. They can't buy that stock for millions of people, there's not enough to go around. So the product they sell is in short supply and is reserved for the big clients. How can they possibly tell you and millions of others to all buy the good companies when there's not enough to go around?

So there's your answer. They know that an index fund is something they can sell to millions of people, and they say this is the only strategy that works. Sure, it's the only strategy that works for them.

The guy on the phone in the cubicle is calling you and a lot of other people and he's basically just a salesman selling those 'safe' index funds. And if he wasn't

working for that brokerage firm as a salesman, he'd probably be out selling aluminum siding or something - he didn't get an advanced degree in investment. But the trading floor looks very different. Those guys know exactly what they're doing, finding specific things to invest in.

Once you really think that through, then you understand that you want to invest like these guys. But the good news is, you don't really have to do that kind of work because you don't have to invest $100 billion. Only your money, and only after you've practiced it over and over and absolutely know what you're doing. This is capitalism. And don't worry... I'm going to show you a lot of the places that you can go to do the research.

Back when I managed a lot of money, we had a Bloomberg machine subscription. All the big firms have one and all the newsrooms have theirs. It's about $70,000 a year to subscribe, but it's got every imaginable bit of information you want. It has every news report from Reuters and everybody else. Not only does it have every bit of general economic information, but also every bit of information that there is about every company that's listed on the stock exchange, the info that's filed with the government -they've got all the information on that Bloomberg machine. So when I retired and went to Florida, I was only going to be investing my own money, and I was thinking gee, do I really need this $70,000 subscription? I mean I had always done a lot of my own original research, but that Bloomberg machine was very handy. And I had people that were helping with the details of all this work.

But the fact is that in 2010 when I retired and went to Florida, I realized that I hadn't been doing a lot of original strategies for the last ten or fifteen years, and things were still working very well. And so I didn't really need that very powerful research tool just for myself. And I found that pretty much everything I was getting from Bloomberg was now posted on the internet. It wasn't all in one place, but it was easy enough to find and I could get it either free or for very little money.

I started to think about when I was on The Closing Bell on CNBC with Maria Bartiromo. One of the guys that was on with me was the senior editor, Phil Orlando. He was the chief editor of Value Line, a publication that talks a lot about specific companies. And I never really thought he knew that much about whether and when it was a good idea to invest in this company or that one.

But I spent a lot of time with him because we were frequently in the green room together waiting to go on, so we talked a lot. And I was amazed to find out that he was doing at least one of the same things that I was doing. I'd either go myself or sometimes send interns to build relationships with the company execs to try to find out what they were planning. I learned a lot about the companies, but anyway I was amazed to find out that Phil was also sending analysts over to try to build those same relationships.

I saw that to a large degree, his information agreed with mine. So in 2011, when I was deciding to do my own research, I went and looked up Value Line. And of course it was very useful; it had terrific information on it. And so I subscribed to it. I forget what I paid, maybe six or eight or even ten thousand a year… but it wasn't seventy thousand! So one day I'm in the library, and I asked for some help to find Value Line, when the lady at the desk said, "You know, you can actually do this online from home, because you can log in as long as you have a library card."

So I stopped paying for Value Line. Instead, I used my library card while I was in Miami, then I moved and they also had it in Sarasota, they have it in Houston, they have it in Los Angeles, they have it everywhere that I've ever looked. Which means it's readily available to you. And in my classes, I teach my students exactly how to use it and how it works.

This is just one example… there's a lot more. And Value Line even has a narrative on every company they report on, and there are thousands of them. They do a report every quarter, and when you read it you'll come to understand exactly what the companies are doing.

What are the changes that are taking place? What are the executives doing? Who's lining up to be the next CEO? What's the competition doing? When you read this whole narrative, you're going to know everything about a company that you could want to know. And you're going to be one of the foremost authorities on this company.

Secrets of the Super Rich

Well, OK, maybe it's not a bunch of 'secrets'. With this 'digital transformation', there really aren't many secrets left, are there? But I do want to tell you how they escape from the herd. This is not about the people who are born super rich; we're talking about the people who become super rich because of what they do. The poor people like to think that rich people got lucky and inherited or by some other means just fell into the money. In my experience, about 80% of people who become rich did not inherit it or get lucky. They earned it by doing something that people care about, that people might need. And they didn't just do it once; they were able to sustain it for years. And then they were able to just keep adding to it.

So many of them invented something new and created a business and were entrepreneurs and showed all kinds of ingenuity. But most of the people who become really rich don't get that way because they personally did something special. They get rich because they use their capital to finance something important, something people care about and value.

What follows now in this chapter are answers I have given over the years. I have been in financial media for thirty-plus years, and I have been investing for nearly sixty years. People have frequently asked me how I made so much money. Most people know that I started in the projects in a family that really didn't have any money. They had brains. And my grandfather knew that it was brains that were going to get me out of the projects; probably not athletics, (which is what I thought was gonna happen).

The fact is, usually the people who ask, have no idea how much money I have, but they can see that I'm able to do what I want when I want, and that I've always been able to do that. And note again that I have not really worked a day in my life with the exception of my time in the Marine Corps. I was a pretty bright kid who got to hang around on the floor of the New York Stock Exchange for several years when all the other kids my age were going out for intramural sports.

But I was always thinking of using my brains to get ahead, to create some power and some wealth and some flexibility and the ability to have a life that I wanted. To have children that grow up much better than I did. I wanted to live in decent places, drive decent cars, and support a wonderful woman who I didn't know yet, but hoped to meet. (And by the way, I was lucky enough to actually meet her and as of this writing, stay married to her for 36 years).

So these are some nuggets or pearls of wisdom, whatever you want to call them, that I've picked up along the way by being around a lot of really smart people, smart businessmen, and smart investors. So you ask why it's been relatively easy for me to support myself and move up in power, wealth, and fame. Number one, it's easy for me to see where the money is, where the money lies, and to understand the macro changes that are happening in the economy… and to see them pretty early in the game.

One of the smartest guys I've ever known, and an old mentor, is Dr. Arthur Laffer. He was one of the top advisors to President Ronald Reagan, and he was the guy who essentially popularized (and I think invented) supply side economics. He was the architect of saving the American economy and creating prosperity. And he did it during a period of time when people like Jimmy Carter (and others) were running the country into the ground.

Now this is very relevant to this moment as I'm writing this book (the summer of 2021), when a bunch of dopey people in charge are duplicating a lot of the stupid things that happened under Jimmy Carter. Fortunately, it didn't completely destroy our economy because this economy is based on freedom. It's so resilient and so powerful that it can redeem itself and save itself from almost any condition.

And by the way, I believe that is exactly what it's going to do over the next few years, even though the present government and the dummies in charge are repeating the actions of the Carter era. And if you don't know who I mean, it's the people in charge of the central bank, the Treasury, the economic policies of the government, the party in control of the House of Representatives and Senate - yes, them!

Well, that was my editorial. But back to this idea that it's easy for me to see where the money is and to understand the macro changes in the economy. And back also to what I learned from Dr. Arthur Laffer. He made an enormous distinction that I hadn't really thought about before, and which almost no one thinks about, and it is exactly what the party in power is doing wrong today, in 2021.

What they are doing is what Dr. Laffer used to call 'static analysis. He called it that in order to distinguish it from what he called 'dynamic analysis'. Let me explain these two concepts. Imagine a party who wants things to be fair. They're not worried about things being fair at the starting line; they want things to be fairer at the finish line. That means they want to decide who's going to win and who's going to lose, and they want to decide who's going to get what.

Of course, our free-market system has produced the most successful society that has ever existed in history. Our incentive system is such that people are rewarded for taking risks, and having ingenuity, financing companies that do things that people care about and want and need. So when the government feels that it's not fair, and they want to make adjustments in static analysis, where you just follow your emotions, they just do what they think will feel good. So when they are of the opinion that one person doesn't have enough money, and another person has too much money, they simply take the money from the one who has it and give it to the ones who don't.

That's what we call static analysis. You make an analysis of the situation and you make the most direct change that's going to make the world the way you want it to be. Now, dynamic analysis is the opposite of that. Dynamic analysis is where you understand that when you make a change, the more powerful people that have resources are going to do what they can to make their lives as good as possible. They aren't going to let you simply manipulate them and change the outcome to your liking. Not only are they smart and have resources, but they're also not really stuck. So they take steps to protect themselves from the changes that you're trying to force on them.

I can give you many examples of this dynamic analysis. That is, understanding that people are going to take steps to make things come out the way they want. And the smarter and more ingenious they are, and the more resources they have, the better they're going to be able to do that.

The simplest example is, if you think I have too much money and you think other people don't have enough money, you just raise the taxes on whatever I'm doing. That way you can take the money from me and send it to them. That's what they mean by static analysis. Well maybe they don't realize or consider that I have some really good attorneys. And I've got a lot of ingenuity myself. And I'm going to think about what I can do to protect myself from you just jacking up my taxes and taking the money and giving it to somebody else.

I'm going to use my ingenuity and get as much smart legal advice as I can. I'll probably find some tax shelters and write offs that are going to reduce my taxes.

Another thing I might do is to move some part of my business to another country. Like for instance a country that's more hospitable to me and doesn't want to punitively tax me.

Imagine that I'm a car company and you want to tax me more, so you raise my taxes. I could simply create a tire factory in another country that has very low or no corporate taxes, and then I make the tires for my cars there, and charge very high prices for the tires.

The company that makes the tires is in that favorable tax environment, charging astronomical prices for the tires. My car company counts those tires as an expense, writes them off, and pays those astronomical prices to my company with the very favorable tax situation. So a lot of the profit ends up in that country with the low taxes instead of occurring here in this country, where you want to tax me punitively.

I can give you a better example that's actually happening right now. It's meant to be punitive and harmful to people who make a lot of money, but as long as we use our ingenuity, it isn't really going to work out that way. Forget about the way the government and the central bank and the Treasury are describing the situation. They say there is very little inflation. They say maybe it's accelerating but it's fleeting, and it's going to go away. And they say that they've been trying to create two percent inflation for a long time and that inflation has actually been running below two percent. This of course, is a lie. (Oooh, there's another one.)

You only have to look at your cost of living to know that even if you're only slightly affluent and have any discretionary money at all - you can easily see that your cost of living has been going up at more than five percent a year for as long as you can remember. Oh, there may have been a couple of years of recession, where prices didn't go up. But for the most part, you've been in a world where the rate of inflation (the rate of decline in the value of the dollar) was somewhere between five percent and double digits. Consider the fact that gold hasn't changed at all, there's still the same amount of gold that there ever was - nothing has happened to change it.

But when Richard Nixon was president gold was at thirty-five dollars an ounce, and now it's at eighteen hundred dollars an ounce! It isn't that gold has changed so much; it's that the value of the dollar has declined so much. Imagine... you need eighteen hundred dollars to buy an ounce of gold - the same ounce of gold that you could've bought for thirty-five dollars in nineteen seventy-two, when the dollar was more valuable

You see we've had a very slow economy, particularly under President Obama. We had a recession, and we should expect periodic recessions. But in 2008, that recession happened because there was a bank crash and a bond crash. The Fed was worried about inflation and raised the interest rates, and all of the big banks had bought mortgage bonds on credit and they thought that they were 'speculating' and making a lot of money on these Fannie Mae's and Ginnie Mae's that were supporting the mortgages.

We believed that everybody deserved a house, including the poor in minority neighborhoods. We wanted it to be equally easy for them to have a house. The rationale was that since houses keep getting more valuable, there's no risk anyway - even if the bank gives a mortgage to a guy who really can't afford that house. And so if the guy doesn't pay the mortgage, they'll just foreclose. There's plenty of security.

Now, what they didn't realize was that when the Fed started to jack up the interest rate, the housing prices started to come down. And what they saw as security to cover those mortgages wasn't really a hundred percent security anymore. The banks had bought bonds from Fannie Mae and Ginnie Mae. There were all kinds of derivative bonds, some of them were paying nine, ten, even eleven percent.

These were very good deals. And the bank could borrow money at four or five percent - they had a lot of leverage and they went and bought these mortgage bonds. They really threw caution to the wind. Just knowing they were Fannie Maes and Ginnie Maes, they felt very safe.

So they bought these bonds. Now, they were supposed to be 'Triple A' rated bonds because they were backed by mortgages on real estate. But when the real estate declined in value, those bonds started to decline in value. They didn't become worthless, and people didn't actually default on the mortgages… but the bond that used to be a thousand-dollar bond and had a great yield on it? That bond declined in value, and it was now only worth maybe eight hundred and fifty dollars. Well, it hasn't foreclosed, hasn't really failed. But if the bank borrowed 95% of the money, and only had 5% of their own money in there, and the Bond went down in value by 15%, then the bank was triple underwater. And if they had their whole net worth (or more) in those bonds, they were way in trouble. They had to be bailed out. And that was the crash of 2008.

What happened was that before they got their bailouts, the banks were starting to fall apart. They couldn't even trust each other - they weren't going to go bankrupt! And people that wanted to buy things on credit - they not only didn't trust the buyer, now they didn't even trust the bank!

Things just went from bad to worse, because at that time we were doing a lot of trade with China. We were buying gigantic containers of goods from them. And if the Chinese bank couldn't trust the importer who wanted to buy that container of stuff, it was because they didn't really trust the guy's bank. Imagine!

The Chinese bank didn't trust the American bank - how were they to know whether the importer's bank was solvent or insolvent? Citigroup was insolvent. Country Wide Mortgage was insolvent. So the Chinese exporter had this trust issue, and they wouldn't send the stuff. Everything started to break down and we had a huge recession. So where was the opportunity there?

Well few, if any, actually realized this was all happening. After five years of prosperity and success, investors, central bankers, regulators - nobody I know of noticed that the banks were going to be in trouble because they were over-leveraged. If you paid attention, you might have seen that the whole banking system was becoming insolvent based on the falling value of the collateral.

The bonds were listed as Triple-A because they were government agency credits, but they really weren't. The quality of those bonds was much lower than the ratings implied. They were rated Triple-A based on the fact that they were issued by Fannie Mae and Ginnie Mae, both created by the U.S. Government, and because the bonds were mortgage bonds, theoretically secured by the value of the mortgaged houses.

We all knew that real estate always went up in value because the supply was finite. All of those assumptions proved wrong. The demand for homes declined because the mortgage rates went up, the economy softened, and as the value of the underlying houses declined, the value of the collateral standing behind those mortgage bonds also declined. They really didn't deserve those Triple-A ratings. They were assigned stupidly by agencies that didn't really care.

The banks were speculating on those bonds and were using huge leverage. Citigroup, for example, was buying those Triple-A bonds with borrowed money. They used around 3% of their own money and borrowed 97%. They were allowed to do it, because those bonds were supposedly a "sure thing."

When the value of the collateral dropped, the prices of the mortgage bonds dropped a little – from $1,000 a bond to around $850 a bond. Imagine if you had bought billions of dollars – your entire net worth – of those bonds using 97% borrowed money, and they suddenly lost $150 per bond. You only had $30 of equity, so you were 500% insolvent. These were our strongest banks, and eventually they had to be bailed out, because our whole banking system was underwater. This was a monumental miscalculation by the banks, the regulators, the rating agencies - by everyone.

Who could believe that the government, the Central Bank, the top bankers, the Congress, the bond market – everyone got it so wrong, and our whole banking system was insolvent? Suddenly, normal business deals we all took for granted didn't work. Chinese exporters who would send a container of goods to an American importer based on a letter of credit from his American bank, couldn't trust the letter of credit, because they had no way to know if that U.S. bank was solvent or not. When the parties can't trust each other, all business based on credit and trust breaks down and a lot of global business grinds to a halt.

Everyone who saw this happening early on was able to protect, sell, or hedge his stock holdings. The Financial Planners and Stockbrokers who wanted to keep their clients told them not to worry, because these problems pass. It wasn't true. If you held on, your stocks lost 50% or more of their value, and you spent the next several years hoping to get even. The problem was that all your money was caught in that debacle, and you were not able to take advantage of the very cheap prices that became available for the stocks of very high-quality companies whose stocks were caught in that pervasive Bear Market.

Seeing economic problems in advance is not very easy but studying the supply and demand for stocks is much more effective. Our Market Xray – which measures longer-term supply and demand for stocks – saw the weakness building throughout 2008 (even though we didn't know why it was happening at the time), and we were able to gradually reduce our exposure to stocks.

That meant we had plenty of cash to buy those top-quality stocks at a huge discount when the adjustments were made – the banks bailed out and the economy was on the mend, around the spring of 2009. At that time, stocks of great companies were for sale at half price, and the millions of formerly over-confident investors now had no free cash, and little or no interest in the stock market. It took many of them years to be lured back in. Those are the same investors caught over-confidently trying to hold onto their already highly appreciated stock holdings after a year of terrific gains throughout 2020.

THINGS ARE DOWN? MAKE MONEY ANYWAY!

Things are down? Make money anyway!

Now, of course when the stock market is falling, it takes everything down with it. So if you realize that you're in a bear market, you can easily find the worst companies, the ones who are having poor sales and you can sell them short. That means you can borrow the stock from your broker and sell it. And it is so easy to make money doing that, because everything is going down and you can just pick the worst companies. Now, an even easier way to do it is to buy a put option – that's an option that allows you to sell the stock at an assigned price.

When the stock actually goes lower than that price, you can make a fortune because you're using terrific leverage. If you were a smart investor, that's what you'd do. But more importantly, even the investor who's not particularly sophisticated may not feel-good betting on the downside. A lot of people feel like that, but it's actually the same either way. But I'll tell you, there's nothing more fun than watching those companies as the economy starts to recover. It happened in the spring of 2009… we were watching the economy getting ready to recover, and the ability to find companies like Microsoft or MasterCard is not rocket science.

These companies are connected to people doing a lot of business, people who have plenty of money and are perfectly positioned – they're already winners, spreading themselves around the world. These are companies that are going to do more and more business as the economy recovers. Buying stock in companies like that could make you a fortune. And if you know how to buy long term options (the right to buy those stocks at a certain price), you could actually be making forty, fifty, even sixty times your money!

With all that in mind, I want to talk a little about what's going on right now as I'm writing, which again is the summer of 2021. By the time you read this book, a lot of this may have already come to pass. But it will be a terrific lesson for you because these kinds of things happen over and over again. Remember, this idea is about your ability to see the macro changes in the economy pretty early. It's an ability to understand how people are going to react to different influences. So let's talk about what's happening in 2021.

The volatility in the stock market in the summer of 2021 was crazy. We had just come through a horrible shut-down of the strongest economy in the world because of COVID. Back in March of 2000, everything crashed. The economy crashed, the stock market crashed, and the recovery was fabulously profitable for everyone who recognized what was happening, particularly in the spring. Then, going into the summer, those who saw that we could manage COVID knew that we were going to get ahead of it. We knew that people were going to get back to buying and traveling and manufacturing and that the world was going to recover.

That digital transformation that started before COVID was going to resume… people in India would again focus on getting electricity and urbanizing and living more like we do. All of that was going to resume and it was obvious in the spring and summer of 2020. So if you recognized that, you were able to buy long term options… it's what we call Golden Rule investing in the companies that produce stuff that everybody wants. And they do it profitably. They own the intellectual property and they're very difficult to compete with. They find it very easy to raise the money to expand. Banks want to lend them money. And if you were really smart, you could actually buy long term multi-year options on those companies.

We're not talking about trading options and guessing what they're going to do next week or next month. I'm talking about buying an option on a company that I know is going to be worth a lot more money two or three years from now. I don't have to know what that stock is going to do next week or next month. What I do know is that 100% of the time when a company is worth more because it makes more money for its owners, sooner or later, the stock reflects that. Sure, they fluctuate, and you can't predict week by week what's going to happen - that's what dopey traders try to do. But I've been doing this for 60 years. I know nobody can get rich by guessing or being a day trader.

At any rate, we knew that the economy of the world was going to recover. Different countries were going to recover at different paces, but everything was going to recover, and that's exactly what happened. We were able to make lots and lots of money. But the momentum started to break down as the growth of the US economy accelerated, and stocks were getting higher and higher. And people were making more and more money and the momentum was building.

Well, the stocks were starting to be fairly expensive compared to how much money each company was actually making. You had very good companies that had a very good future, but they were selling for thirty, forty, fifty times their revenues, not times their profit, but times their revenues. Obviously the company was going to continue to grow. But it was getting to the point where it was going to take years for them to catch up. So that stock wasn't such a good deal.

Now, it's a fact that when the economy was growing faster, the rate of growth was also accelerating. The Stock Market tends to key off the rate of change of the economy, not so much whether the economy is growing or not. So going into 2021, all of that momentum had built up and companies were going for thirty, forty, fifty times their sales. And then the rate of acceleration of the US economy started to slow. The economy had been growing at seven percent, and then it went to eight percent, then nine percent. The stock market was reflecting all this and everybody's making a fortune.

Suddenly in February or March, it seemed like manufacturing that was growing at eight percent began to drop off, now growing at seven percent, then six… and you might say yeah, but it's still higher than it was last month. Why isn't it going up? Because as I've said, the investors key off the rate of change. With that kind of a momentum, it happens all the time.

You're learning about it now. And you're going to see it happen many times in your life. But the rate of change started to decelerate; it's happening now in the U.S. economy, and it's starting to happen in the global economy. So we can see that the demand for stocks is starting to weaken, the same way as it was in early 2008.

As a smart investor, when we start to see that volatility build and the demand for stocks start to weaken, we begin to divest. We start to protect ourselves, protect our portfolio, and we start to have less exposure to the stock market. And we love when this happens. Because here we are with companies that are growing and actually making more profit this month than they made last month. The rate of change is not accelerating. The stock price of that company is coming down. Meanwhile the company is actually growing its sales and growing its profits.

Now watch this… as the stock price falls, and the company continues to become more and more valuable, eventually we get to the point where it's a really good deal! And we're able to buy in again and make a fortune again! So we love this cycle. And we love to see the stock price falling as the company becomes increasingly valuable. They still make something that people want and need, and they're the very best at it… they're very difficult to compete with.

Again, we're talking about companies like MasterCard, Visa, Microsoft, and Twilio. Remember, these are platforms that companies like Amazon and Netflix are built on… platforms that allow them to reach the whole world. There's more and more demand for those companies but the stocks have stopped going up and are really starting to roll over. And this is that fabulous opportunity period.

Basic Ways of Thinking About the Market

Let's start this section by understanding what's going on in the stock market. First, it's not behaving like it did last year. We made a lot of money last year and I really liked the way it was. But it's not really being that odd or unusual right now; it's just not the same as the way it was - but it's getting ready to offer us a terrific opportunity. We had great opportunities in March, April and going into the summer of 2020.

We're going to get another run at a similar opportunity. But I wanted you to see what's going on here - we're looking at stocks like Microsoft, Visa, MasterCard, and Amazon. So I have this chart showing these and they're long-term pictures of stocks that have fluctuated wildly.

The people that were trying to figure out what they were going to do from day to day, week to week, or month to month, were frustrated and generally lost money. And yet everybody knew these companies were getting more and more valuable, because they were reaching more and more people, and they were very profitable. And yet, lots and lots of people managed to lose money trying to invest in them. So let's look at the big picture.

Because there are millions of people trying to participate in the markets as investors, pretty much everything is priced right. That means there's no real opportunity for you to make a lot of money. Lots of people are buying, lots of people are selling, and they're agreeing on the prices. That's the free economy. So if the world thinks something is too cheap, then everybody tries to buy it and they bid the price up. If something's too expensive, they sell it and they knock the price down. So there's not much in terms of opportunity for an investor.

In order for you to make money, you have to find things that are mispriced. A simpler way of saying this is, for you to make money in the stock market, somebody has to be making a mistake. Now if you understand this, you're half-way to where you want to be - if what you want to be is a successful investor. People are afraid of the stock market, because they try to participate in it by using magic instead of using common sense. The reality is, if you think in terms of years, you have a very good chance to make money owning companies like these. And because most people can't think in terms of years, either because they don't know how, they don't know they should, or they're incapable of it, they'll make a lot of mistakes by focusing on what they see short term and what they hear on television. And often they're going to misprice things, giving you some great opportunities.

That's what happened in March of 2020, when everybody panicked about COVID. By looking at the short term, everything shut down and everybody stopped making money. But what we understood was that sooner or later, the world was going to get past COVID. By nature of the fact that the whole world joined together to do the research was inevitably going to work and the world was going to get past it and move on. We've been marching forward and progressing for a million years. That progression has accelerated for 100,000 years and even more so for the last 100 years - in the past ten or fifteen years it's hard to measure how fast we've progressed. It's become pretty clear that we'll beat COVID.

The reality of the free economy is you are rewarded for doing things people want and need. And that's what I call Golden Rule investing. It's simply a strategy that works. Golden Rule investing isn't working because we have such nice people. It's because in our economy, you always get rewarded for doing things that people care about, that gives them a better life - and that's what they're after anyway. They're going to go for it with you or without you. So the most powerful and reliable strategy as an investor is simple: you identify a few things that people want and are committed to get, and then position yourself as an owner of the companies that provide those things. Essentially, they'll be buying those things from you.

The skill involved is to identify the companies that are not only doing the right things, but to find the companies that are doing them better than everybody else, using techniques that are very difficult to copy because of their intellectual property. Then all you have to do is know how to analyze the company and make sure it's profitable. That's when it becomes worth owning.

I know. There's a lot to this. But successful investing is actually pretty simple. Note that I said simple, not easy. Observers who don't know what they're doing are worried because they feel that the stock market's risky and unpredictable. The truth is companies that profitably create a growing clientele of people who want to buy their stuff - their customer list continues to grow, as do their sales and profits. And they continue to make more money.

One hundred percent of the time, with a little patience, companies that make more money and become more profitable eventually see it reflected in their stock prices. Not sometimes, always. So why are so many people afraid of the stock market? All you have to do is learn this stuff. I'm committed to teaching as many people as possible the means to do this. In fact, I even offer a free workshop to explain how my classes work, and people love it… mostly they're just amazed that it works so well. (You can check it out at www.themoneyman. com)

Next, I want you to understand the herd of lemmings and how they behave. Is the term 'lemmings' an insult? You know, I guess it is. But it was smart to understand that while the herd of lemmings was panicking back in March of 2020, it wasn't the end of the world. Humanity was going to continue its march forward. And that was a wonderful opportunity to buy great long-term investments on sale. Like fashion bathing suits in the winter, they are fabulous, but not everybody wants them right then.

So who's doing the selling in the stock market? Well, the stock market is having a lot of selling, though it doesn't feel good to everyone. Most of the herd members thought about it but were paralyzed by fear. A large number of them didn't join in until November or December of 2020. Remember, we started investing in these companies knowing that there was going to be recovery. But we started doing this back in March, April, and May of 2020. We knew that eventually, sometime in the summer, it would hit a lot of people that the world was going to get past the pandemic.

There was a nice rally that started in November, and some people made money. But these late comers were underwater in a lot of their holdings. And in true lemming fashion, they're only praying to get even, so they invest for self esteem and not money. That's why they're thinking that way. This has value for us as a textbook demonstration of what not to do. But also, as a particular company (or sector) sees its stock rise in price, there are a large number of late comers who sell just as soon as they get even on their investment.

There were people who were buying into the stocks on which we had already made a fortune. They heard about it and wanted to join and here it was already October and November of 2020. They joined, and now they're underwater. I'm explaining what's going wrong with the stock market, it starts to rally. And then as your particular company goes up, and they're not all going up together, but as a particular company sees its stock go up, it rallies a little bit. And then all of a sudden, people are selling it. What's wrong? Well, they started late. They were underwater, saying to themselves, "Damn, if

I could only get even… I'll stop smoking, I'll lose weight; I'll be kind to everyone". Then when they do get even, they sell! So what's going on in the stock market? With the S&P 500 at an all time high, why would you and I agree that the market's not feeling so good?

It's because only half the stocks on the New York Stock Exchange are even in a short-term uptrend. I'm looking at the percentage of companies above their 10-day moving average, which is only a bit more than half of them. In a short-term uptrend, half the companies are not in a short-term uptrend, they're in a downtrend.

This is something that we've been watching forever. But this is the number of companies advancing versus the number of companies declining on the New York Stock Exchange. And for the stock market to be at an all time high, assuming the S&P 500 meant what it's supposed to mean, and if these indexes were giving a true picture of what's going on in the market, then of course, there would be a lot of companies advancing and very few companies declining.

We reached the peak of the number of advancing versus declining issues a few months ago. And since that time, the ratio has been getting worse. The number of declining issues is going up, and the number of advancing issues is going down. It's amazing that this is happening in a stock market where the S&P is at a record high. All this says is that there are a lot of companies going up, but there are a lot of companies going down.

I'm looking now at a little longer time frame. It's the percentage of stocks that are above their thirty-day moving average. And you see only about half of them are in a moderate medium-term uptrend. Over a 30-day moving average there are still as many companies that are in a downtrend as an uptrend. So the market is weaker than it looks on the surface. I'll give you some examples. General Motors says they have the lowest inventory at their dealerships that they've had in many, many years. There's tremendous demand, and yet, the stock is going down.

Of course, we understand that their production is interfered with because they need computer chips, but that shortage is temporary. This is a company that over the next couple of years is going to have record sales and profits. Look at this. I'm looking at GM's earnings per share growing at thirteen and a half percent over the next five years. You haven't seen that happen with General Motors for a long, long time. This is a company that's going to be increasingly valuable, with a return on equity of twenty percent - and yet the stock is being sold!

Here's another one...Toll Brothers. I look at our record demand for houses, there's almost no inventory, and the prices are great. The companies are selling all the houses they can get, and business is fabulous. And yet, even as the prospect for profits for these companies is terrific - their stock is declining. Notice that this is happening with the S&P 500 at an all-time high earnings per share.

Next year, we're going to be up over forty percent, with a seventeen or eighteen percent gain on earnings per share for the next five years. And yet, next year's price to earnings ratio... I don't want to get too technical, but this company is selling at seven times this coming year's earning. Seven - not thirty, not fifty.... seven!

Royal Caribbean says that they have just as many orders and just as many deposits on cruises now as they had in 2019. Everybody wants to go on cruises. And yet they're nearly giving them away. I know they are because I recently got a bargain on a cruise. They're giving them away just trying to get people back. And people are doing it. The company has always been profitable, and it's just a matter of time. So this is a company where you have the opportunity to make a fortune.

So what's going to happen now (remember now is the summer of 2021)? Well, we're about to have an infrastructure bill and the infrastructure bill that's now proposed is basically about things like steel and aluminum. See, the rebuilding of the bridges and highways and buildings was already in the cart. We knew this was going to happen. We've already made a lot of money on these companies.

Now we're going to get another chance at a bargain, because short sighted investors are going to be selling while Nancy Pelosi is trying to indicate that they won't pass the infrastructure bill. You see, they're watching and reacting to the news. They watch this week's news, next week's news, and even next month's news, and that's how they decide what to invest in.

They don't really know what they're investing in, they're just following each other; it's a herd. Nancy Pelosi postures that they're not going to pass this bill, but it's inevitable that it's going to happen. You and I know that the United States is going to fix its bridges and roads. Everybody agrees it needs to be done. Everybody wants it done. Democrats and Republicans in the Senate passed it and if Nancy Pelosi doesn't pass it, somebody else will in the next Congress. The country is going to repair and build bridges and roads.

Now, the more they sell the stocks over this story, the better it is for us. And it's very likely that we're going to see a tremendous bargain on companies like Cleveland Cliffs natural resources, because undoubtedly, Nancy Pelosi is going to posture and make believe she's not going to pass the infrastructure bill. So this is the short term picture of these companies. Is it not obvious that the current government is willing to print any amount of money to do the things that it wants to do?

Look at companies like Nucor. Is that stock going to be in trouble... is it going to sell off? No! Nucor is going to have earnings per share growing at twenty-seven or twenty- eight percent a year for the next five years. Actually, earnings per share over the last five years have grown at sixty percent per year because the price of steel has been moving up. Cleveland Cliffs' earnings per share are also forecast to gain close to twenty-eight percent earnings per share over the next five years. There's going to be an enormous amount of profit made. And while it's likely that you could probably make money if you bought it now, if you wait a little while you're going to get that bargain.

I want to show you the kind of money that you could make doing this when you use a little bit of leverage... and a little bit of your brain. We saw what was going to happen with copper. Everything they want to do in the United States includes building windmills, building electric cars (which take four times as much copper), they want to redo the grid, etc. In India, you have a billion and a half people, and a billion of them don't have electricity. They already have the grid to their villages.

But for now and the near future, they're completely distracted by COVID. Right now they're doing nothing. But as they get past that, they're going to be running copper from the step-down transformers out on the pole, finally to the homes of all these people. That's going to mean an enormous demand for copper, all over the next several years.

If you'd bought options on copper back, say a year ago, you made forty times your money. That's by simply knowing how to use leverage. Back in April of 2020, the stock price for Freeport McMoran copper was at eight dollars and eighty-five cents a share. We bought multi year options, so that we would have the right to buy it at seventeen. Why would we want the right to buy it at seventeen when the stock was at eight? Because we wanted to use a lot of leverage, we wanted to own a lot of that company. The stock was at eight eighty-five, yet the option to buy it at seventeen was available at thirty-three cents per share. So we were able to buy a lot of it.

That was April 2020. By January 2021, the stock was at a little over thirty dollars. Do the math... that thirty-three cent option was now worth over thirteen dollars. You get the picture? That's around forty times your money. So that's how you use leverage for a company that you want to own. So you own a lot of it; you own as much of it as you possibly can.

I've had a lot of questions about Continental Resources. Why is that stock falling? What's wrong with it? Isn't the world going to need more and more oil and gas? And aren't they in a perfect position? Isn't the company profitable with oil at thirty-five dollars? This was in the mid seventies. You've seen it fall from the mid seventies down into the sixties. The company's enormously profitable with oil at sixty-five or seventy dollars, and you're probably eventually going to see it at a hundred dollars or more, but for the moment, we've made the money. Remember, back in April of 2020 Continental Resources was at $8. We've made the money on that.

So now we're sitting here waiting and watching the stock sell off and watching investors worried about the media frenzy. The media just loves COVID-medicine-vaccine stories. And they just keep talking about it. And you get so inundated with that story that you start to think that way. But this is not a short-term investment.

This is a world that someday may or may not get past carbon fuels, but in the meantime, it's going to take an enormous amount of oil and gas, and for many years it'll be the kind of resource that's going to be the most profitable. And now we're lining up for another terrific opportunity. If the stock market does have a correction, it's going to be a terrific opportunity. And as you're beginning to learn, we'll be able to make a fortune on Continental Resources again.

In the meantime, take a look at Chevron, a perfect example. It doesn't matter what the stock does; they're perfectly positioned. They have a lot of upstream position. They find the oil and drill for it, they get it out of the ground, then they transport it, then they refine it. They're in a perfect position. And they're probably the most profitable of companies that do this.

By the way, Exxon's dividend is probably close to six percent as well. These are companies that are going to provide you with a place to keep your money. It's not about speculating on when the stock is going to go up. These companies over the years are going to be worth more and more money; there is no question about that.

MORE COMING AS
WE SPEAK!

More Coming as We Speak!

T here are enormous opportunities that are opening as I'm doing this book. Things change of course, so let me add my disclaimer… this book was started around the middle of August of 2021. And boy, the stock market's been absolutely fabulous since March of 2020. That's when the fabulous opportunities came, because the markets crashed as though the world was coming to an end. And of course, it wasn't.

We knew we'd get past COVID. The whole world figured that out by the summer. So the value of companies that are associated with getting people what they want and need - the value of those companies started to rise because the sales were increasing. They developed vaccines, and by November of 2020, it became clear that those vaccines worked. They were something like ninety or ninety-five percent effective. That, obviously, was a tremendous boost for our emotions, and the stock market started to run up again.

As I'm writing, it's become clear that we've already had a gigantic acceleration here in the American economy. And now it's a question of just getting back to work and the economy getting back to something we think of as normal. And bang, all of a sudden, new variants of COVID show up.

As you know, the media love to tell you stories about how many people aren't getting vaccinated and how we'll never get rid of COVID, how we'll never reach herd immunity. They report that these people aren't getting the vaccine, and those other people aren't getting it either, or this vaccine works better than that one… they love it because it's a way for them to get your attention.

It's baffling but true that people love to hear more about these COVID vaccines, and particularly how bad things are. So now there's this view here that the central bank is going to begin to caper the support they've been giving to the economy. And meanwhile, people have been buying more and more and starting to travel and go out to eat and drink and retail sales have been increasing, all at an accelerated rate. But now it's sort of getting back to normal, where we have normal growth.

Now, rather than try to explain why people do what they do, I can simply tell you that today, our market X ray is showing underlying weakness. It's not a bear market. But we're having what I call divergences. I don't want to get too technical, but what's happening is when the S&P gets to an all-time high, as it recently did, you'd think there'd be an all-time high in the number of companies that are advancing. That would be consistent with a stock market that's going up. And meanwhile, the number of declining issues would be shrinking. That's what our market X ray generally shows.

Those indicators are very good for telling us what's going on beneath the surface. And right now, beneath the surface, the stock market has been getting weaker and weaker. And meanwhile, the S&P 500, which is being run by just a few big companies, is making new highs every other day. Those companies generally are going through what they call a rotation.

What happens is that, for a couple of days, these 'new technology' companies go up, and everything else goes down. And then those companies begin to go down. And the industrial companies that are all about rebuilding the economy, including the copper mines, steel mines, and manufacturing companies... well, they start to go up. And they go up for a few days, and just like a bunch of lemmings, they all start following each other. They really don't know what they're investing in, they just follow each other. Now those stocks start to run up, and what do you think happens next? (Hang on, it's a speeding merry-go-round).

As those sectors run up, the companies with the new digital transformation technologies, and the cool new ideas and the medicines that were going up last week, they start to go down. There isn't actually a coherent bull market rally going on. Instead, you have this rotation, with more stocks going down than going up - all this in spite of the fact that the indexes are frequently hitting new highs… it's very confusing.

A lot of investors just lose interest because they can't figure out what to invest in. First the thing they're buying goes up, and then they find out that the other thing is going up. So they sell and they buy and they follow each other. But they're just running around playing musical chairs, they're not making money.

And suddenly the world is going to figure out that COVID is just a matter of time, it's going to be a thing of the past, and we get on with rebuilding our lives. And then we get a coherent stock market rally with the index going up, and more companies going up than going down. And more companies hitting new highs and more upside volume. And all of those things that are consistent in a bull market, they just start to happen. And so we resume having real demand, and it becomes easy to invest because we've got a couple of more years of rebuilding.

There's another thing, and it's gonna make you a lot of money if you just understand it and take advantage of it. It's about all this money printing they've been doing, pouring it into the economy and sending it to people trying to support the economy. That was a good thing to do back in the summer of 2020. But it hasn't been a good thing to do since the economy has been recovering.

Many people didn't need all this free money, but the government's been run by a new administration, and they want to buy votes. They want to spend a lot of money on infrastructure, which would be good, but that doesn't mean they should just send money to the people who vote for them. The people who vote for them are generally the people who don't make a lot of money, who don't have good businesses.

In fact, the people who had to stay home because of COVID tend to be the poorly paid hourly workers. The people who had a good business took the opportunity to work from home. The people that had a special profession also got to work from home. Their income really didn't see a big interruption, unlike the lower paid hourly workers who just have to show up in order to get paid.

I'm talking about the people who mow your lawn or collect the garbage, the low paid workers at the office, the prison guards and all those people who can't 'phone it in' - they have to show up. And so when things slow down, when whatever they're doing slows down because of COVID or whatever else, they lose their income, and they're in trouble. They're the ones who vote for the Democrats.

And so there is a concerted desire now to keep printing more and more money, and to keep sending it to those people, to finance their stay-at-home attitude. But when you print trillions and trillions of dollars, the obvious result it that you have a dollar that's not very scarce. And it's compounded by the fact that it's not just the U.S. printing money. When the Japanese print trillions of dollars worth of the Yen, and the Europeans do it with the Euro, and the British do it with Pounds, and the Chinese do it with Yuan, there's so much paper money around, the value of that paper money goes down. Because we think in dollars, to us it looks like everything else is going up. And that's the way it's going to be.

What's a good way for you to get rich? You can invest money in anything they can't simply print, anything that's scarce and in demand, any thing that people need to get the lifestyle they want. You can invest in companies that provide that. And you should, because those companies have pricing power; they can raise their prices, they can adjust for inflation, they become more and more valuable. And what they do becomes more and more valuable.

So the more these guys flood the economy with money, they're making the money they print worth less. The good news is they make the things that are in demand worth more, especially when the companies producing those things are the best at doing it. It also helps if there isn't a lot of competition and their product is in big demand.

Let me explain what I mean when I say these people have pricing power, and that they can adjust and raise their prices even with a little bit of inflation. Example; if inflation is rising at three percent a month for a company that provides a platform that Amazon is built on, a platform that helps Amazon to get to you by some means, let's say your telephone… if it's a platform that Amazon's built on, they can raise the price of that by a couple of percent a month.

Amazon is in a position to keep up; their stock is going to keep up with inflation. It looks like their stock is going up - what's really happening is the value of your currency, the value of your dollar, is going down. This means your savings are getting less valuable, and your safe investments in bonds are getting less valuable. So you can make a fortune by investing wisely in these premier companies.
By the way, these guys are helping you make even more money by making the dollar worth less, making everything you can't print worth more - you have this fabulous opportunity facing you right now.

So we know the trick is to pick out a couple of companies that are doing things that people really need. I keep going back to it, because it's a perfect example – it's the companies that provide copper and steel. The world is going to rebuild, and that means tons of copper and steel to build new high rises. The United States is going to build all kinds of infrastructure; we're going to rewire our grid, just as they're going to rewire the grid in India and China. It's all happening, using tons of copper to do it. And for the electric cars that they want to build and that they want to use - those electric cars use four times as much copper as a gasoline driven car does. So demand for copper is going to be enormous.

We're getting a tremendous break in that the price of copper has gone down tremendously. The stock for Freeport McMoran, the copper mining company is actually going down. And because temporarily, China has been letting a lot of its copper reserves go because they couldn't stand how fast the price of copper was going up. And so technically, you can see that the price of copper, which is around four dollars as I'm writing this… it was at four fifty just a while ago. The reason is because China is selling off a little bit of their copper.

But in order for them to grow, they're gonna have to buy it all back. They know it. They're just trying to mitigate the inflation. Right now, it's irrelevant. And people around you are afraid that the economy is going to slow because some place in the Midwest has more COVID cases, and South Dakota and California have more COVID cases… this stuff is all temporary, short time baloney!

Over the next few years, all the things we want are going to use more copper. The value of that Freeport McMoran stock is going to be much higher than it is today. This sell off is temporary because people have lost confidence in the short run. I'm going to bet on it going down and watch how much money they're going to make. We're gonna have to buy the copper to do what they want, and then we'll own it, and let them buy that copper from us. Over the next several years, we can make a lot of money. That's what Golden Rule investing is about.

Let me go back to 2010. At that time the CEO of Google was a guy by the name of Eric Schmidt. He pointed out that in the time frame between the dawn of civilization through the year 2003, there was a certain amount of data that had been created. It was estimated at five exabytes. If you don't know what an exabyte is, it's equal to a billion gigabytes. Let's just say it's a lot of data. Then back in 2010, Schmidt stated that this same amount of data had been created in a period of just two days! Wait, there's more. In 2020, we created fifty-nine zeta bytes of data. So let's see, that's about fifty-nine thousand exabytes… holy cow, that's a trillion gigabytes.

So it took from the dawn of civilization to 2003, to create five exabytes of data, and by 2020 we were creating that same amount of data every forty-five minutes. This is something that we and the rest of the world are doing, and we just can't seem to stop. There's not a country on the planet that can't embrace this. And all the uncertainty that surrounds you is actually coming from the fact that you're trying to figure out how fast this stuff is going to continue to happen. It comes from being very short-sighted and looking at things under a microscope.

Infrastructure for the digital transformation of the world; it's happening region by region, rich countries first, poor countries last. But poor countries know that they can't become rich without embracing this better way of doing things. They can't. But to understand it requires a lot of vision, which most people don't have. Remember that most investors are just following each other and trying to guess what each other is going to do by using charts. Folks, the ability and desire to actually understand what you're investing in takes effort. You can't predict what the crowd of gamblers is going to do this month based on patterns on a chart.

One way to invest is to know what real values will eventually be. And the other way is to try to guess what the herd's gonna do - whether they're going to follow each other into a new pattern or be turned away at the support or resistance levels. And as I've described, any idiot can see those levels on the chart, but who knows if they're going to bounce off of it, or fly right through it?

Yes, it's true that it's so much easier to guess what's going to happen than to actually use your brain and do some relevant research. Which of course, appeals to the wishful thinkers who want to make money without knowing anything... they wish there was a chart that would make them rich.

This is why there's no such thing as a rich 'technical' trader. You know there was an old friend by the name of Wayne Root who frequented our radio program as a guest. Some years ago, he actually ran for president. He didn't even come close, but running for president helped him become famous, and it helped his completely counterfeit business (sorry Wayne, but no one will see this except my readers). You see, Wayne had the most expensive pay-per-call 900 number in United States telemarketing history. It was $100 a call to get Wayne Root's sports betting advice, and millions called in to get those handicapping numbers.

You have to understand that handicapping is not about who's going to win the game... most real fans have a pretty good idea of which team is better. But you have to understand that the market changes the odds, the market set odds, and depending on how many people are betting on one team, they change the odds and give points to the other team. So if the Red team is a favorite to win (everybody knows they're the better team), they give the Blue team enough points to make it even. The odds are adjusted so that the known factors are already figured into the odds.

When Wayne Root gives you advice on which team to bet on, he's saying you should gamble against the odds. Wayne's giving you advice on how to beat the odds, which is absolutely nothing more than a pure gambling game. Nobody knows what the outcome of the game's going to be. Wayne hasn't got a clue, nobody does. If the bettors knew for one second what Wayne Root thought, then the betters would adjust the odds according to what Wayne thought, and it wouldn't be valid anymore. So he made a lot of money on dumb wishful thinkers who paid a hundred bucks per call for his advice on how to gamble on the games.

Now this folks, is what technical analysis in the stock market is… picking the odds of a company breaking out of resistance or being turned back, or that chart makes no difference at all - because the situation probably just changed and a chart showing you the past tells you nothing. Any way you select, there's no way to tell which one you're looking at. And that's why you're never going to find a rich technical trader, other than somebody who makes a lot of money by teaching wishful thinkers about the support and resistance levels, and the technical pattern myths.

It proves that if you wanted to go into the business of teaching people how to trade these patterns, you really don't have to know very much. You just have to be good at writing ads, spend some money on Twitter and FaceBook, get yourself a 900 number, and talk a good game.

Now, I'm about to tell you about a few companies and I need to make this disclaimer… I don't know if these companies are going to start going up today, or whether some of them went up last week, or whether they're going to start going up in a month. I don't know this, and I really don't care – I just want to make my point.

What I do know is that if a company is becoming more valuable because it sells something that people feel they've gotta have in order to have the life they want, then that company is making more money for its owners. That means the people who bought stock and own a piece of that company, their stock is now worth more money than what they paid for it. This happens every single time.

Eventually, and in the not-too-distant future, the company stock moves higher. This happens 100% of the time, folks. So if you know what you're investing in, it's because you took the time and effort to learn about the company and know what you're doing. The stock market is not a gambling game. It is a brain game.

This brings me to the point of this discussion, which is that there are a number of companies who are leaders, and they're the best providers of behind-the-scenes infrastructure that it takes to allow the world to compete. Everyone wants to complete the digital transformation that's been going on for several years; it's the future of the world.

These companies create the platforms and the infrastructure that it takes for broadcasters and providers to reach the customers who are sitting there eagerly waiting to spend money with them. We're talking about the customers who are dying to buy things on Amazon and dying to watch programs and respond to advertising on Roku. They sign into their TD Ameritrade account, and they get a number via text which they then fill in on the website. They're using a platform that ties together the text, internet, telephone, and all these different media on one place. It's all built on the Twilio platform.

Here in the United States, we're so used to all this sophisticated stuff that we don't even notice the infrastructure that allows Netflix and Hulu and Amazon to work, we don't notice it. We forget that if we wanted to watch a movie on Netflix a few years ago, it took a half hour to load while we were content to watch a spinning clock or a progress bar on the screen. That was okay back then, but not now. And why isn't this happening now? Why is it I get instant communication with Amazon and with just a few clicks, I can have a new pair of running shoes delivered tomorrow?

If you've been following my work, or if you understand the concepts in this book, you know a lot about these companies. The platforms that Amazon and Netflix are built on, like Twilio and Cloud Flare and Fastly, these are companies that make possible the next generation of the worldwide web. I include in that list Nvidia, Shopify, and more recently, Digital Ocean. It gets pretty detailed, but you always have an open invitation to join me for free information, podcasts, and even workshops via my website. Take a minute to check it out at www. themoneyman.com

It's Your Turn, Now!

I've talked about the media a little bit in this book because unfortunately they play a major role in the way people live and think. Now, they've been joined by the big banks, the government and everyone else who has an agenda for you and your money, and the whole bunch of them are keeping you down and losing you money.

It's not that their plan is to keep you poor, it's just that they don't care if what they say is keeping you from getting ahead. Mainly the media are trying to entertain you or hold your attention until the next set of commercials comes around, and the financial guys are just wanting a piece of your money.

Now, I know this to be true because I spent my life in newsrooms. I saw it happening firsthand because I spent my life talking about money on both radio and television. I saw investors getting stuck. I was born poor, but I was never stuck, because I was always thinking about what I might do to get ahead.

I've mentioned that my grandfather explained to me that the secret wasn't some gimmick. It was his realization when he came over from Russia that the U.S. was set up so that if you do things that people want, and you help them get what they want, you get enormous rewards and the sky's the limit. I understood this, and I've always played the game accordingly.

I wrote a book about ten or fifteen years ago about the fact that everything was getting globalized. We had all the gifts here in the United States, and everybody wanted to copy us. We had gone from three hundred million people to two or three billion. (Now we're in the range of eight billion!) And so, our big companies got rich, and people around the globe began to live more and more like us. Global trade was growing, and everything became more efficient. If one country was particularly good at manufacturing, everybody did their manufacturing there. And America was very good at inventing things and using energy and optimizing the use of oil and gas, so we got to be more and more productive and produce more and more stuff.

The story 10 years ago was that because business got so good and international trade opened up so much, the big companies suddenly had bigger markets, and you could invest in those companies. You didn't really have to know anything, and yet you could make ten, twelve, fifteen percent a year and you'd gradually grow. And that's what my radio and television programs were about - and I was fine with that. I wasn't really interested in poor people who didn't have a lot of money because we were managing big money. You had to have at least several hundred thousand and preferably millions in order for me to make money by managing yours – I mean I could only charge one or two percent, right?

So we did a lot of programs that were aimed at the common folks. But those folks could invest in these big companies and make a good return, and eventually have enough money and earn some leisure time. Everybody was happy. And honestly, I never really thought about it. That wasn't what I wanted

Made in the USA
Columbia, SC
01 June 2022

61178570R00095